MW01114501

BORN TO MULTIPLY

LASHAWNE HOLLAND

authorHOUSE®

AuthorHouse™
1663 Liberty Drive
Bloomington, IN 47403
www.authorhouse.com
Phone: 1 (800) 839-8640

Published by AuthorHouse 05/09/2019

ISBN: 978-1-7283-0939-2 (sc)
ISBN: 978-1-7283-0938-5 (hc)
ISBN: 978-1-7283-0937-8 (e)

Library of Congress Control Number: 2019904933

Print information available on the last page.

This book is printed on acid-free paper.

Because of the dynamic nature of the Internet, any web addresses or links contained in this book may have changed since publication and may no longer be valid. The views expressed in this work are solely those of the author and do not necessarily reflect the views of the publisher, and the publisher hereby disclaims any responsibility for them.

Born to Multiply may be purchased in bulk for educational, business, or promotional use. For information, please contact www.LaShawneHolland.com

I dedicate this book to six very important people in my life. Without your love, encouragement, support, and loyalty – none of this would be possible.

To my four heartbeats:

Robert,

Everyday I wake up, I thank God that you found me. You have been the most amazing husband, friend, supporter, provider, protector, father, and business partner. I thank God that we get to build and do life together. Thank you for loving me past my imperfections and protecting my heart when other shots arrows in it. My very best friend…until the end of time.

Your Weekend Girl

Adam

My first born…son of my youth. I remember the moment I looked at you on the day you were born and I remember thinking "I didn't know it was possible to love something so small, so much, so quickly and so completely." You truly were blessed with wisdom beyond your years and I am so honored I get to watch you share with the world, what I already knew while carrying you in my belly…. you were born to be great!

P.S. You are really the co-author of this book. It would NOT have been completed if you didn't push me, spend countless hours reading, editing, re-structuring sections. You truly are my ride or live partner!

Jonathan

My favorite middle son. I often think when God blessed me with you, He reached into His heart and out came you. The day you were born and the first time the doctor laid you on my chest, you looked up and smiled. You have been such a joy to raise and watch as you grow into an amazing young man. You are so full of love and compassion and I am so full every time I see your smiling face. I love you beyond words. I am so proud to be called Mom by you. Never allow border bullies to steal your dreams because they were placed in your heart by God Himself. Your superpower is LOVE. Never let life cause you to let go of it. Its your gift. God placed you here on earth to share it with the world. Now, go be great!

Zoe Lynn

My favorite daughter. My baby girl. My mini-me. You are the dream come true that I never knew I had until you were born. Your love, affection and kindness has changed my life in so many ways. I love our relationship. Our friendship. I love our Saturday trips to the grocery store (*wink, wink) and our deep conversations. I love how you see the world in color and live life on your terms. I love your independence, your loyalty, your boldness, your kindness and your benevolent spirit. Your generosity is admirable. I love you so much and I pray blue diamonds, pearls, sapphires, rubies, jadeites, musgravites and emeralds are in your future and on your balance sheet. ☺

Together, WE ARE THE HOUSE OF HOLLAND!

To my Pastors, Tony & Cynthia Brazelton

"Thank you" seems so minuscule when compared to what you have done for me. I was a sophomore in college when I met you and in so many ways, I feel like you have raised me in the faith. Your love and influence have shaped my thinking, you have transferred your faith to me and it has taught me to use faith in the places in life where my natural eyes couldn't see. Pastor Tony, you are the most amazing visionary the world has ever known. So many times, you have been my eyes when I couldn't see my calling. You helped birth it in the earth. You guys are the midwife to my dreams and calling. My life and the lives of my family would look so different if I never crossed your path and I am forever grateful to God for leading me to the Brazelton's. There is no greater influence on my marriage than your example of what God intended marriage to look like in the earth. Pastor Cynthia – you taught me how to love my children without conditions just by watching you with your kids. I remember the first time I heard you talk about putting love notes in your kids lunch and at that moment, I vowed I would be that mother who never left her kids to question her love for them. I think I've done an amazing job myself ☺ but it was by your example that this was possible.

Growing up, I never saw a happy, successful marriage. You created that image for me. No one ever took the time to tell me God wanted me wealthy – you created that image for me. I never knew it was possible to be a friend of God – you showed me it was possible. Thank you for teaching me how to reach into eternity and bring Gods best for me to the earth. I love you guys eternally. XOXOXOXOXO

CONTENTS

FOREWORD BY APOSTLE TONY BRAZELTON

It was around '92 or '93 when my wife and I first met LaShawne. Still in college. We had just started a church, and she would come to service whenever she was back home on break from school. From the beginning, we could see that God had called her to the world. For her reach to go further than the church. We were just privileged just to have her come back to work with us. It was so exciting to see her evolve. How she went out into the business world, studied, learned, and succeeded. Then brought those lessons back to the kingdom. I feel privileged to have observed her from a unique perspective. Every day, I continue to see her walk in her calling, from a bird's eye view. That awesome, far-reaching calling I first saw on her as a young college student. She closes the gap between her current self, and her destined self every day. But I also see her from a ground level view, because she's my daughter. I see her heart, her passion, her drive. I see that every day. But it all began with that day in my office. With God showing me what He was calling her to do. And I remember asking her "Hey when you go to school don't you forget come back and work for your Dad." I remember that day well.

The first impact that LaShawne has had on me, and by extension all those that our ministry has touched, is that she took us from this mom and pop financial mentality to shaping this incredible financial culture in our ministry. Things were so informal, but kingdom requires structure. That strong financial organization and structure is what we are now operating in today. That's one of the first shifts that I noticed, and that shift took place immediately.

I believe she will continue to shape and transform how people see money, from a kingdom perspective. I believe that LaShawne is a product and embodiment of our church's creed – anytime you can see the word, hear the word and understand the word of God, you can be converted to that word you see, hear and understand. She is a living, breathing, embodiment of that creed. She has taken the principles of prosperity that we have preached and she has absolutely become the WORD made flesh. That word dwells not only within LaShawne, but it's manifested in the life of her family. Her children walk in the reality of God's desire to prosper people. She's doing things that her natural family has never seen before and that's just a product of the word. And the thing that has been so good and powerful about LaShawne is that she is a word person. She loves God. She has always loved God. She loves His word. She takes the word in. She is a doer of the word. And so, one of the things that we see in her life is that she is an absolute example of the vision of VCMI. It is one thing to go to church. To hear the word. But it is a different level, and one that we aim for, where you become that word. Then for that same anointing to be transmitted generationally in her family. It's amazing to see.

LaShawne is all about that transformation into what the word says we can have and be, financially. So, another impact that she has had, when I think about all that she does for the kingdom, has been a manifestation of God's word. Her impact has not just been on her Mother and I as her spiritual parents, but for the kingdom itself. She is so helpful to a lot of other ministries. She does her due diligence to make sure that we're always on the cutting edge, always handling our financial affairs in excellence. She is also able to take what God has put in my heart and shown me a vision for, and she creates a tangible strategy to make that vision a reality. We just pass her a dream, and she knows from a legal, investment, developmental, financial standpoint how to make it happen. There have been times when we just pass her what heaven says and then she will carry that out - she puts legs to a thing and make the means work so that we can reach that end. We show her the destination, and she draws a map. Having LaShawne on this team has always given us the confidence that we could do it, and do it again because we have someone like her that can put together means together to give spiritual people earthly direction.

So, her impact is just nothing short of amazing. God called LaShawne to this financial arena. This is what her Mom (Pastor Cynthia Brazelton) and I saw when we looked at her. We saw God endowing her with the gift to use her financial and business knowledge to materialize in the natural world what has already been ordained in the supernatural. To change the course of human history for churches, businesses, everyday people, anybody who would just be open enough to receive it.

The thing that really blesses me the most about LaShawne is that she isn't someone who is just telling people principles that she hasn't walked out herself. She has absolutely walked these things out. I think this book stands as a testimony to that as it incorporates three important things that I think are extremely necessary for God's children to prosper: wisdom, knowledge, and understanding.

Everything she does is with the aim of positioning people to do what she has done. To help them move into a place of financial freedom. Her life is a testimony of how to prosper during this time in human history. Not only does she possess knowledge, through years of self-education and experience, but she has wisdom. Wisdom is the ability to effectively and strategically wield the knowledge that you have to leverage the most you can from it, given the world around you. She knows how to take what is in her hands infuse it with her wisdom, knowledge, and understanding, and watch it transform into something that was already destined in the heavenly realm. She has done it all her life, and this book really gives you a window into those experiences for those that weren't there to see them first-hand like I was.

By reading this book, I think the number one thing that people will get is the wisdom of God. The supernatural understanding that the world needs. They will also receive the knowledge they need to be able to have the financial freedom they desire. The financial breakthrough they need to transition into their wealth as well as whatever God has called them to be a part of as their personal destiny in the earth. A scripture comes to mind to help me explain what I'm talking about – in Proverbs 24:3 (NIV) which says "By Wisdom a house is built, and through understanding it is established". Another translation says that by wisdom a house is built, but knowledge fills its rooms with fair and beautiful treasures. I believe that is what LaShawne brings to the table.

I believe that she brings knowledge, which is simply information, wisdom which is the application of the knowledge, and then she has understanding, which is experience. She brings all three of those components to help people move from where they are (scarcity and unbelief) to the place that they desire (financial freedom and wealth generation). So, I would encourage everybody to read this book for a lot of reasons. But the one that comes to mind is that there is a spirit of mammon (the false object of worship) out here in the world today, and so many people are unaware of it and its effect on humanity. People are making so many decisions that are governed by mammon and not governed by a kingdom reality.

LaShawne has the gift to arrange things in their proper place. To reignite the belief that what is in the supernatural can be materialized, and you can use the knowledge of the natural world to do it. LaShawne has proven that she can thrive in a Christian structure and a non- Christian structure. She is a bridge. We know that the spirit of mammon wants to take the place of God – to tell you that you don't need God, all you need is money. We know that someone can have money and be totally unhappy. Money magnifies your problems, your vices. It doesn't make them go away. It can't replace God. So, open this book, and receive the wisdom, knowledge, and understanding to be able to move in those areas that LaShawne has dominated. The areas of business, finance, entrepreneurship, investment, the areas that God has called her to work in. Open this book and learn how to master your money, instead of being a servant to it. Open this book, make the effort to apply its principles, and I guarantee you will begin to experience Heaven's reality.

-Apostle Tony Brazelton

AUTHOR'S NOTE

As a man thinketh, so is he. I had broke thinking, and I was broke. My journey didn't start yesterday. And it won't end tomorrow. Many people see me with my family on stages around the country (and internationally) and think that I was an overnight success. My success, however, has been anything but quick. My climb has been over two decades in the making. I think the hardest part of the journey—harder than actually walking through the doors of businesses, harder than being the only African American female (at times) in the rooms on Wall Street, harder than sending my kids to schools where the cost of tuition was over $1.3 million BEFORE college, harder than having to forgive the people who have stolen from me and taken my kindness for a weakness, harder than losing money in the real estate crash, harder than losing money to crooks who swindle people with false claims of returns on investments called Ponzi schemes—looking back, the hardest part of my journey was transforming my financial blueprint, my money mindset, my generational programming of bad money habits, and the process to reconstruct my financial DNA.

I have learned that oftentimes, when you are a trailblazer or a bridge-builder, there is no model for you to follow. You have to take out the machete and swing it in every direction you know how. You have to cut down the weeds of fear, disappointment, and the hurt of people backbiting you—even people from your own family. You have to cut down the weeds of bad financial habits, the weeds of debt, and the weeds of unprofitable actions. You have to cut down the fear of success and the fear of failure. You have to cut down the weeds of receiving bad financial advice.

See, I have been working on my mindset for years. I have learned that every new level requires you to have a new way of thinking, a new playbook, a new coach, a new insight, a new skill set, and new strategies.

And it hasn't been easy. There were so many nights on which my husband Rob and I would lay awake in bed and stare at the ceiling in the dark. We didn't want to say out loud what we were feeling because we didn't want any negative words to counteract the affirmations we were speaking about over and over in our daily lives. We didn't dare murmur and complain about not having enough because we had learned that wealth isn't attracted to negative language or thinking. We would hold hands and nod at each other, trying to reassure each other that God was well able to supply all our needs, even if we couldn't see how He was going to do it.

We have made lots of money. We have lost lots of money. We have made it back. Once you know the blueprint for financial mastery, it's easy to replenish funds. But the hardest part of the journey was transforming our money mindsets. Now, I spend countless hours teaching, coaching, and leading people to what's possible with financial freedom, financial independence, and financial security. So often, people don't even realize that the programming that they received as children affects how they handle their finances in adulthood. This is especially true in the church. We think that just because we are born again, that our money gets born again too. Listen, if you had bad credit when you went to the altar to be saved, you will still have bad credit when you get back to your seat. We can shout, declare, pray, and do somersaults across the stage, but until you change the way you think about money, you will never change the way you live.

My grandfather used to say, "What you do in moderation, your kids will grow up to do in excess." I find this to be truer now than I ever have. This is why debt levels are at an all-time high. People are stressed out, feeling like they are financially suffocating, feeling unworthy of wealth and abundance, accepting what society gives them as the final say, and living life in financial bondage. My assignment is to tell you to send that blueprint back to hell, to open your eyes and see what's possible, to live the life you were created to have—a life with choices and options. But you can't see what's possible when you think like a slave.

See, our money blueprints can go back five generations. Depending on your age, African Americans living up to five generations before you were slaves. We have traded in one form of slavery for another. Financial bondage and mental slavery are a strong representation of the physical slavery we endured in the 1800s. True financial freedom isn't about not having credit card debt or zero student loan debt or no car note. I know plenty of people who don't have any credit cards with an 800+ credit score, and they aren't financially free or living a life of wealth and abundance. The number-one reason they live this way is that they still think like slaves. Imagine that: in the 21st century, we are still thinking like slaves.

Building wealth requires you to think and act like a free man. We can't move ahead because of the shackles on our minds, and the sad part is we don't even know those shackles are there. I didn't know it. I didn't realize when I was filling out credit card applications and charging it for stuff that I no ability to repay while I was in college, that I was thinking like a slave. I didn't realize that when I was shopping, filling up my closet instead of filling up my savings account or investing, that I was thinking like a slave. Think about it. Find the correlation between post-slavery bondage and how we handle our money in today's world. We are programmed to be renters and not owners, to be consumers and not producers. We buy liabilities instead of assets. Just look at the statistics to be reminded how far behind we are.

Now, a lot of it is no fault of our own. African Americans got a late start in many things, and we still have a long way to go in closing the wealth gap in the United States. But I am talking about the things you CAN control, like living off 100% of your income. As slaves, we were not allowed to own property. So, today, it's not a priority for us to be PRODUCERS and OWNERS instead of modern-day sharecroppers and slaves. We were not allowed to own life insurance policies. The slave owners were legally allowed to insure their slaves against the untimely death of one of his human "assets," but today, we see no value in helping the next generation NOT start from ground zero by investing in life insurance. Our thinking is, if we can't drive it, wear it, or see it sparkle, we fail to see the value in investing our money in it. We were not allowed to own assets, so today—even though, according to Target Market News, we have the spending power of $1.2 trillion—we are still way behind in asset accumulation. We weren't allowed to read. And now that we can, only 30% of African Americans will pick up a book to read and invest in their personal development to create the life we truly desire. That means there are 12 million African Americans who haven't read a book in the past 12 months.

We weren't allowed to vote, so we had no voice in our communities, state, or nation. Now that we can vote, we don't show up to the polls. Slaves didn't have wills or estate plans. Slaves had no head in the state, no name, title, or register, nor could they take these by purchase or descent; they had no heirs and, therefore, could make no will. Whatever they acquired was their master's. When you die without an estate plan, you die intestate, meaning the state you live in gets everything. Only 36% of Americans have wills, but when you consider just the African American community, the numbers are far worse: Less than 20% of our demographic invest in planning for future generations. Then we get mad when people don't contribute to our GoFundMe campaigns. I often tell people, "Don't have your family crying for two reasons: that you're dead AND that you left them broke."

Slavery was hereditary and was intended to be perpetual, meaning it was intended to last across generations. PLANNED CAPTIVITY, just like our monetary system in the US, was designed to teach us to be credit rich and cash poor. Think about why they offer us department store credit cards at checkout; the worse kind of credit to have on your credit report is department store credit. It's credit for liabilities, not assets. SLAVERY was never intended to end. They may have physically freed blacks in 1863, but they just created multiple other units of slavery that were made possible by mentally enslaving us and programming us to be inferior, not to have economic dominance, economic equality, equal playing fields, or the ability to gain access to capital to grow businesses at the same rate as white business owners.

Slaves weren't allowed to protect themselves. The Bible says that money is a form of defense. Society has rigged the system so that blacks are not on the same playing field as whites. Subprime loans, difficulty in financing for business ventures, planned ghettos, unfair housing opportunities, etc.—all of these things are set up to make it virtually impossible for blacks to get ahead.

Slaves were not allowed to wear clothes finer than "Negro cloth." This is the root cause of African Americans feeling the need to impress people by dressing in the latest trends and designer clothing: They want to be seen as "worthy" of more than "Negro cloths." So, we spend money on looking good instead of BEING good. We sacrifice our future wealth-growing potential for a new outfit every payday. My grandpa used to say, "If it's on your a**, it's not an asset." I like to use version 2.0 of his saying: If your a** is wearing it, driving it, or walking in it, it's not an asset.

Expecting people to work and conduct a service for you without intending to pay them is a form of programming that has its roots in slavery. Slaves were not allowed to be paid. The Slave Codes of 1705 prohibited slaves to be paid for labor. IT IS A SLAVE MENTALITY TO EXPECT PEOPLE TO WORK FOR LOW OR NO WAGES. When you constantly ask someone to render their goods or services to you for free, you are displaying a slave mentality.

Slaves weren't allowed to own businesses or create environments for economic gain. Today, we would rather stay on jobs we hate and continue to be underemployed or stuck in positions that don't pay us according to the value we add to companies. Why? Because we have been programmed to stay in less-than-favorable conditions no matter what it costs us.

Slaves were not allowed to save money. Even post-slavery, blacks couldn't have savings accounts or bank accounts. Today, 7% of blacks (3 million people) still don't have bank accounts. There are also "underbanked households," whose residents have a bank account but still elect to use services like check cashing, money transfers, payday loans, and pawnshops. The percentage of the black population living in underbanked households is 19.9% (that's over 7 million people).

Slaves didn't have a plan to be free! After they were freed in 1863, many didn't want to leave the plantations they worked on. Poverty was widespread among the black population because they no longer received food rations, nor did they have places to live. They wanted freedom but didn't PLAN for freedom. The same goes on today with money. People want more money, and they claim they want financial freedom, but they don't have a plan for their financial freedom. They don't see the value in learning about money mastery, creating business systems, or investing. Black bodies were capital, but blacks themselves could not control capital. They had to be laborers. That feeling lingered long after slavery ended.

For you to change your economic environment, you need a new playbook, a new mindset, and a new blueprint. This is why I have written this book, to show you what's possible. If God can take a girl who grew up in Pomonkey, Maryland to two teenage parents and help her to defy the statistics, put herself through college, build wealth, and change what wealth looks like for her kids and grandkids (remember, a wise person leaves an inheritance to his or her children's children), it's possible for you to do it too! However, for you to unlock wealth, you must start thinking differently. Thinking like a money master isn't optional. You must defy societal statistics and racial and socio-economic divides. You must believe that WEALTH IS POSSIBLE and know that WEALTH IS POSSIBLE FOR YOU. So, accept the fact that YOU WERE BORN TO MULTIPLY!

INTRODUCTION

"Overcoming poverty is not a task of charity, it is an act of justice. Like Slavery and Apartheid, poverty is not natural. It is man-made and it can be overcome and eradicated by the actions of human beings. Sometimes it falls on a generation to be great. YOU can be that great generation. Let your greatness blossom." – Nelson Mandella

I was supposed to be a statistic. That's the reality. I did not have anything set up for me. I'm not a trust fund baby. I have never hit the lottery. I wasn't born to C-suite parents with ivy league educations who positioned me to graduate from college and walk into a multimillion-dollar corporation. That's not my story. I was born to an 18-year-old father and a 16-year-old mother, without a silver spoon in sight.

Although I was born to teen parents, my early life circumstances were still far from what you see in the movies. I always had food on the table. I never went to bed hungry. Even if my food was grits and potato salad (which I hate to this day, because we ate it all the time), I always had food, shelter, shoes, and clothes. So, I don't want to paint the picture that we lived in a drug-infested neighborhood and that I was dodging bullets on the walk to school. That isn't my experience. But that doesn't mean that the living standard I experienced wasn't a form of poverty.

Now, some of you reading this may be able to relate to this story. Others may have been born into opportunity. Some of you may be reading this thinking, "Honey, your childhood sounds like a cake walk compared to mine," and it very well may have been. I still had a lot to be thankful for growing up, and life could have been much worse. We all have our own story. The most important thing in life is that it is never too late to rewrite your story.

Imagine being born with a bright young mind and a promising future. Your talent shows at an early age, as you begin speaking at six months and walking at one year. Then, at 19 months, you contract a mysterious illness that leaves you without hearing and sight. What was beginning to sound like the beginning of a positive and inspirational story suddenly becomes the plot of a tragic tale. Who cares if you showed promise if you can't see or hear? You will never see a work of art. You will never hear the birds chirping or the beautiful sounds of music. What do you have to live for? How in the world could you work past that? Well, someone did. This brave woman moved beyond adversity that would cause most to give up without remorse, and few could criticize them for it, given the circumstances.

Her name was Helen Keller, and she went on to not only be the first deaf-blind person to earn a Bachelor of Arts degree, but she also co-founded the ACLU and went on to be one of the 20th century's leading humanitarians. Given the adversity she faced, many would say her hopeless story was written in stone. But she shattered that stone and used it to build the foundation for a legacy that extends far beyond her lifetime and into the history books.

I say all this to illustrate that one of the biggest things that stands in the way of people achieving breakthroughs is their story. Each of us has a story, or maybe multiple stories, that have served to shape our lives up to this point. Our stories are where we are anchored and where our core resides emotionally, mentally, and sometimes even physically. The stories we are anchored to can either weigh us down or propel us upward. It all depends on how you to interpret them, use them, and ultimately change them.

Helen Keller could have simply been the woman who was deaf and blind—she could have let her story define her. Instead, she was the woman who overcame being deaf and blind to become a world-class humanitarian, as she reshaped her story to help define her life and leave an even more epic legacy. There is a stark difference, one that I desperately need you to understand. You can easily be defined by your story when you relinquish your power to your past and your circumstances, when you accept that you are nothing more than what life has presented you with. You are playing blackjack with the cards the house dealt you on the first go-around, and you aren't even bothering to hit and improve your hand.

Imagine you are in a game of blackjack. The dealer starts out dealing everyone the customary two cards. You receive a 2 and a 3. You look around the table. Some look optimistic. Some look just as distraught as you do. The dealer asks everyone what they would like to do: "stay" and keep the cards they have, or "hit" and receive another card in hopes of getting closer to 21. Now, you could choose to focus on the cards you were dealt. You could think to yourself, "I'm so far away from 21, I'll never get there. Everyone here must have a better hand than me; how in the world is my luck so rotten? The dealer has it rigged anyways, and they always win. I'm no expert, and some of these people here have studied and trained their whole lives to become masters of blackjack, while I only know the basics. The bottom line, given all this: Why should I even try?"

Do not look at your story as a chain; look at it as a rope. Would Rocky have been as great of a movie if he never had to work to come back and beat Apollo? If he had never lost in the beginning? Being the underdog only makes your story that much greater. Do not look at the rotten cards you were dealt as the reason why you will never succeed. Look at them as tools you can use to make your success even greater. Use what you were given to forge an epic story.

If I had been born a millionaire, what I have achieved thus far in life would not be very impressive, and many of you would not likely be reading this book. Likewise, you would also not be reading this book if I had let my circumstances define me, if I decided to live the rest of my life as the black girl born to teenage parents who was told she would never accomplish anything. If this were the case, none of you reading this would have ever heard of me, and the world would be indifferent to my existence. Whether you start on level 1 or level 100, what the world remembers is PROGRESS—the distance between where you started and where you finish. No one remembers the rich person who was born rich and remained rich without doing anything to increase or decrease their fortune. No one cares about the poor person who continues to be poor. What the world remembers lies in the middle ground, in what happened between point A and point B. So, do not let your point A define you.

Starting with a 2 and 3 in your hand, how epic would it be if YOU came back and won this game, if you beat out all the people who had trained for this, gone to school for this, had experience in this, were dealt a better hand, as well as the dealer who is favored to win over everyone? You look the dealer right in his eyes, and you say "hit." You take a chance, and you go for it. You work, you grind, you study, you educate yourself, you get smarter, and you strategize. Hit after hit, you see yourself inching up. You've gotten into a rhythm. The others didn't expect you to be in this long. They are getting nervous. The dealer is getting nervous. With all of those cards, you shouldn't still be in it. You must be crazy. You never stood a chance. Suddenly, you're sitting there with 19. Everyone else is "staying." You and the dealer lock eyes one final time, but now, you're seasoned. You have learned through experience, educated yourself, read books, gone to conferences, joined mastermind groups (are we still talking about blackjack?), and you know the odds are in your favor because you've worked too hard for it to be any other way. You hit one last time. The card is a 2. No greater and no less than the sorry 2 you started with, but thanks to your hard work, perseverance, and ingenuity, this 2 and that first 2 have become a part of a story that is so much greater. You yell out "blackjack," run home with your pot, and you invest it in assets like I know you will after reading this book :), and people at the casino are talking about you for weeks to come.

I am not much of a blackjack player (I have actually only played it once in my life when I was in college; I lost my money and never played again), but through this example, you get the idea. Helen Keller would not still be taught about in schools if she had not been met with stiff adversity and then leveraged it. She was not simply a blind-deaf woman; she was a world-class humanitarian who was blind and deaf. She took the weight of a horrible deal, leveraged it, and used it to catapult her legacy much further than it would've gone without it. She took her story, tore it up, and used the bits to create a new story, a historic one.

That is what I did, and that's what I will continue to do with the unfortunate stories that shape me. I was born to teenage parents, and my guidance counselor told me that kids like me don't go to college and that I should take up a trade. And I thought, "How about I trade in both of those stories for a new one? How about I trade the destiny the world expects of me for a new one?" Nothing stops us from being in the history books except for ourselves and the power we give our stories to control us. If your life started better than Helen Keller's, then there is proof right there that there is hope for you. As a matter of fact, when writing this, I mistakenly spelled her named with two *L*s, and spell check corrected me. I WANT SPELLCHECK TO KNOW MY NAME. No, it's not "La-Shawne," "LaShawNEE," "Lashaun," "Lushawn," or "LeSean." It's "LaShawne," and the *S* is capital, just like a dollar sign, baby!

So, sit up straight. Make sure to take notes, highlight, and underline. Most importantly, prepare yourself to actively apply the information, tips, and lessons I plan on teaching you throughout this book. Faith without work is dead. So, commit yourself to practicing what you learn, and get excited, because this is just the beginning of your new story.

CHAPTER 1

The Invisible Box Called Fear

One day, I was washing clothes in my grandmother's basement, and she came and sat down on the steps. As she watched me move the clothes from the washing machine to the dryer, we started talking. She asked me what my biggest dream was. I was confused. She had never talked about dreams before.

Let me give you some background. I was in my senior year of college and had moved in with my grandparents to save money for my upcoming wedding. My grandmother was dying from cancer. She had lived 26 years longer than what the doctors told her she would live. She told me on my wedding night that she prayed that God would allow her to live long enough to see me get married. She died three days after I returned from my honeymoon. God honored her prayer.

But back to the basement story. When my grandmother asked me what my biggest dream was, I stared at her because I didn't have one. I guess it would have been graduating from college. As we continued to talk, she said, "When you decide on it, never let fear keep you back like I did. I was afraid to live my dreams, and now it's too late." That conversation has never left me. We had plenty more like that before she died. We talked just about every day when I would return from class. Oh, how I miss her sage wisdom and unconditional love for her family.

So, in light of my grandmother's conversation with me, I want you to take a second to visualize your ideal life. All of your dreams, including all of your business, financial, relationship, family, and health goals, have been realized. You live in your dream home with an amazing and loving

1

family. You feel healthier in your mind and body than you ever have. Your vitality is beaming through. Your business has grown more than you could have imagined in your wildest dreams. Or, maybe you had no desire to be a business owner, and you work the most spiritually and financially fulfilling job you could ever ask for, and you are well compensated for it. This is the best that life can get. Now, I want to ask you a question. Why are you not there right now? What is stopping you from your ideal vision becoming your reality?

I want you to write the reasons down. Is it your current circumstances? Is it money? Are there more pressing matters which make the present a poor time for working on your goals? Does your spouse not agree with your vision? Do you think you aren't ready to take that next step? Are you too busy to do anything more than what you're already doing? Has something traumatic happened in your life that you still haven't been able to work past? Write down every reason that comes to your head, whether it seems stupid, or shallow, or painful to think about. Get it out and write it down.

No matter what answers you came up with, in some way or another, every single one of the reasons you gave as to why you aren't where you want to be in life is rooted in the invisible box called fear. I don't believe that God wants us to live in fear—actually, I know He doesn't because He said so in the Bible. Yet so many people allow it to rule their movement on Earth. There are so many phobias and fears that exist in society: fear of heights, fear of getting older, fear of spiders, fear of the dark, fear of change, fear of water, fear of speaking in public, and the list goes on and on.

For instance, if you answered, "I don't have the time," you are probably just fearful of wasting your time on something that you're not sure you'll have any success in. Or maybe you're afraid to give up what little free time you have for doing things like scrolling through your phone or watching *Real Housewives*. Maybe you don't think you deserve to be wealthy or to live the life you dream of. That is fear of success, or perhaps a fear of being overwhelmed. Regardless of the reason, if you think about it deeply enough, any reason you can come up with as to why you are not living your ideal life is truly rooted in one form of fear or another.

To begin this journey that I want to help you with, you are going to need to acknowledge your fears for what they are and move past them. This is the first step that you must take before I can begin to work with you to establish a wealthy mindset. The wealthy don't fear success, and they don't fear failure. They do not fear accomplishing their goals or fulfilling their vision. All these fears are trivial and fall by the wayside for these people. I remember reading that Oprah once said, "I have fears. I have just learned to move forward in spite of the fear."

When pursuing the vision people have for their lives, whether it is climbing the corporate ladder, starting a business, or whatever someone's vision may entail, all their reservations boil down to three types of fear, all of which require a different response. The three types of fear are fear of failure, fear of wasting time, and fear of seeming vain.

Fear of Failure

This is a big one. I come across countless people who say they never take that first step towards their dream because they are afraid of failing or because they believe that acquiring great wealth is not possible for them. However, I believe it goes deeper than that. Fear of failure is actually, at its core, simply a fear of being judged by those who matter to us. If you fail at something and there is no one around to judge you, you will simply try again. Sure, you might get discouraged, but you will keep trying and failing to make sure that you truly can't do something before you give up. However, once you have people watching you, it is a completely different story. Your self-doubt amplifies at a much quicker pace, and you get discouraged much faster. Heck, you might not even try.

In such a situation, it's easy to think to yourself things like "Do they think I'm dumb?" "Would they be able to succeed at this even though I keep failing?" "Are they looking down on me because I can't get this right?" "Are they going to tell other people about my inability to get this done?" "Is this actually hard, or is it just hard for me?" Questions like these and hundreds of others can go flooding through your brain. Well, in the age of social media, we experience this fear nonstop. We can't shake the irrational fear that, if we fail, everyone—from that cute guy you met at the mall last week to your high school biology teacher—will know that you failed. Or worse, it will give your church members something to talk about. So, what is the result? It's that most people do not even try.

First off, if you plan to achieve anything great in life, you need to learn

3

to embrace failure (but also don't fall in love with it and purposefully tank at everything you try). I remember my pastor saying something to me once that changed my outlook on failure: "Believers don't fail, we just regroup." So, from that moment, I adopted the idea that we either win or we learn. If you have even the faintest desire to make your life's vision a reality, failure is necessary—it's how we learn what not to do.

As a child, my youngest son, Jonathan, hated vegetables. He swore up and down that he was allergic to anything green and claimed he would throw up and die if he even touched it. This is how some adults react to the idea of failure. They can't even think of getting close to it without feeling nauseous. Just as you need to eat vegetables to grow strong and healthy, you need to experience failure to grow mentally, spiritually, and financially. I have made plenty of bad investments, I have been in mountains of debt, I have had an army of credit cards, and I have made poor financial decisions. But look what those failures have helped turn me into today. The only reason I am here writing this book right now is because of my failures. I went through it, learned from it, and I do my best to pass those lessons on to people like you so you can move more quickly along your path to financial freedom. Let me tell you something: Successful people are also the people who have failed the most but who have also been receptive enough to see the value in their failures. Thomas Edison is an example of this; he once said, "I haven't failed. I have just found 10,000 ways that won't work."

Failure is like a piñata: Once you crack it open, you find some sweet takeaways. Often, knowing what not to do is just as important as knowing what to do. I always tell my kids that in everything in life, either you win, or you learn. It's as simple as that. I have learned quite a lot over the years, and I am grateful for all my failures. I embrace them because they have made me who I am today. They have made me wiser, stronger, more aware, more thankful, and more driven.

So, you see, it is not failure that we should fear, and most people do not fear failure itself. People can follow the logic that, just as a child shouldn't fear vegetables, an adult shouldn't fear failure and should realize that it is good for you and helps you grow. However, just as a child doesn't fear vegetables themselves, people do not fear failure itself. Instead, they fear the bad taste of embarrassment it leaves in their mouth after being judged by those around them whose opinions matter to them.

The wording used here is the key to overcoming this form of fear, so let's break this sentence down to two parts.

The first part of this sentence mentions the embarrassment you feel after being judged by those around you. I want to start this exercise with a revelation that may shock or offend you but which I feel compelled to tell you anyways. You are not that special. People are not laying around glued to their phones looking to see how your life plays out. It may seem like that in your head, but that's simply because humans are egotistical creatures. We always think that everything revolves around us, that everyone is watching us, and that everyone is concerned with what we do. In reality, most people do not care. That popular girl from high school has her own set of problems to worry about. She is trying to put food on the table, deal with a bad ankle she never got looked at, and figure out why her husband comes home smelling like a perfume that she doesn't own. Trust me, the last thing she is thinking about is you!

I don't say this to belittle anyone. I say this because it's true and because I need you to snap out of this mindset. These people are not thinking about you. So, what if you try a business venture and it flops? These people will not remember! The memory of the average American is now three scrolls of the thumb! How many celebrities have accidentally leaked a racy photo, or said something they regretted, or got caught leaving the club with the wrong person? Scandals like this are everywhere in the media for a day at most, and then it's back to your regularly scheduled programming. If people move on that fast from the blunders of the most famous people in the world, imagine how little time they spend focusing on your failures.

The second part of the sentence above touches on those whose opinions matter to you. This portion of the statement is significant because, in life, we tend to give people a lot more of our time and attention than they give us in return. We just covered the fact that most people you are concerned about are not thinking about you. Yet, somehow, we care about each one of our 2,000 friends on Facebook's opinions anyway. Why is that? You see hardly any of these people on a daily basis, and many of them you will probably never see again in your life. Therefore, their opinions should not matter to you! If they are not putting food on your table or money in your pocket, their opinion doesn't matter. If they are not furthering your goals or getting you closer to your vision, their opinion should not matter to you. We devote our time and energy to so many things that don't deserve it, and that is why people have so much anxiety all the time. It is so important to realize that there are people in your life who are supposed to be there only for a season. Do not let a season affect the rest of your life.

Imagine if you literally did this. Imagine that you're insecure about your body, so you get extremely fit for the summer so that everyone can see that you're in shape. Summer comes to an end, and you know no one will see your body in the winter. That would be absurd. But you are so obsessed with this little splinter in time, with the season of summer, that you wear summer clothes year around. You walk around in spandex or your bikini in the winter just to continue to impress everyone and let them know that you haven't slipped and that you're still in shape. You are still maintaining your hourglass shape. Or, if you're a male, you want to walk around with a muscle shirt on year-round to flex your six-pack and biceps. You would not only look ridiculous, but you would also probably die of hypothermia.

The same goes for your dreams, don't leave them out to freeze to death just because of the people who are in your life for just one season. Their opinions don't matter, and you should not allow their opinions plant fear in your heart. Not caring about others' opinions does not mean you are indifferent. It means you are comfortable with being different. There is so much relief in realizing that (1) people do not care about you as much as you think they do and (2) you no longer care about people as much as you used to because these people have no impact on your daily life or on the dreams you hope to accomplish. You have to resolve yourself to not put energy into thoughts that don't deserve it. This will free you up to put your brain power toward things that actually matter, like your financial freedom.

So, my first recommendation for overcoming the fear of failure and the fear of being judged is for you to sit down and make a pact with yourself that you will realize that most of the people in your life do not matter. They are sand on a beach, leaves in the wind. I need you to mean it.

I remember having a conversation with my son when he was torn between working on his business or hanging with his college buddies. I told him that people would not remember that he wasn't at a party one night and that, to be honest, they would not remember him at all a few years down the line. I told him not to live for people who wouldn't remember him. It reminded me of a story of when my son and his friends had a shaved ice business as teenagers and they wanted to go play basketball with their other friends. I didn't have a problem with that, but they had signed a contract to service an event. I made them honor their contract. That evening, after they finished, they were in the basement playing PlayStation or some other gaming system, and I threw $8,000 in cash onto their heads. That's how much they had made that day vending their shaved ice. I said, "Now, tell me who on that basketball court made $8,000 today," and we all laughed. I am pretty sure no one remembered that they were not even there playing basketball with them.

Now, for those people who are close to you and whose opinion you do value, good communication solves most problems as long as you confront your problems head-on. Sit down with the people you care most about and say, "I would like to talk to you about something, and the only thing that has stopped me was my fear of what you'd say. I need to know that I will have your support when I fail (you need to know in the beginning that all business ideas may not pan out, but that doesn't mean you are a failure). Because I will. In one capacity or another, it is inevitable. I will not fail spectacularly, but I definitely will suffer short-term setbacks. Failure is never failure; it's just a regrouping stage. It's part of learning. In the long term, however, I'm going to win, and it would mean the world to me to know you've got my back and are hoping for my success, and not waiting for my failure." Then, no matter how they respond, just start. Do what you have been paralyzed with fear and waited way too long to do and start walking out your vision.

It is a hard thing to hear, but when you start to experience success or even just start to want better for yourself, some people you care about will hurt you. Lord knows I could write a book about this too. Your attempt at growth will cause them to reflect on their own place in life, and if they don't like what they see in the mirror, they can lash out. There will be close friends who try and tear you down. There will be family members who don't support what you are doing. And you know what? That's okay. If they knew the way to financial freedom and true wealth, they'd be there already. It doesn't have to be a scene. You don't have to be disrespectful.

Just recognize once they show their true colors that that is where they stand. You can love them from afar, but other than that, you do not need someone in your life holding you back when you have so much more to offer. Eventually, they might come around and admit that they were wrong. If their pride doesn't allow them to do that, then at least maybe your actions will positively influence them to get up and work to make their lifelong dreams a reality as well.

I am telling you, you will be amazed at how quickly you can work when you're no longer tethered by the tyranny of other people's opinions. Those who are afraid to fail will always set their goals far lower than they need to, much to the benefit of their competition who aim for the stars. No one who played it safe ever made it big. This is your life, and your chances of truly ruining it are slim. There is very little that you can do that you cannot recover from. Be strategic, clear-eyed, and willing to work harder and longer than you ever have in your life, and I guarantee you won't disappoint anyone. In fact, you will probably surprise everyone.

Fear of Wasting Time

This fear affects everyone differently based on their age. Let me start this off by saying that if you are under the age of 40, this should not even be an issue. If you try starting a particular venture or business and you hate it, or it doesn't work out for one reason or another, you can always return to the real world in a couple of months. The 9-5 world will always be there. Every successful entrepreneur has failed. Most have failed many times. Failure is not a waste of time—there is always something to gain from it. Acclaimed author Mark Manson said, "Being wrong opens us up to the possibility of change. Being wrong brings the opportunity for growth." You are young. I guarantee that the time that you may "lose" in a failed venture is more valuable from the standpoint of practical, real-life experience than anything you would have learned in that same time period spent in a classroom or working a job that requires no use of your God-given abilities.

For all of us over the age of 40, and maybe even 30, who have families, tons of bills, and are approaching or past that halfway point in life, our time is a little more valuable. We cannot run around trying this or that because we have people who depend on us. We have to be strategic with how we spend our time. That being said, everyone has downtime. Whether you would like to admit it or not, if you took the time you spent double tapping on Instagram or watching *Love & Hip Hop* and put it toward educating yourself and shifting your mindset to that of a wealthy person, you could already be closer to making that vision we talked about a reality. TV is not an essential, scrolling through Instagram recreationally is not essential, and playing Candy Crush is not essential to you cashing in on your bankable purpose, becoming financially free, or establishing sustainable wealth systems. Take this time and start putting it toward things that you will thank yourself for doing when your time is finally up. Take that free time and start that business. Take that mastermind course on revitalizing your finances. Enroll in that stock-investing institute. Sure, it may cost you a couple of hours of sleep, but you'll have plenty of time to sleep when you're dead. Rob and I worked full-time jobs and came home just to eat dinner and work another work day on our businesses for years. You have to want it. Even if it doesn't work out, and whatever you put your effort toward simply wasn't for you, it's okay. It was worth it because you learned from it. Remember, we have to embrace our failures. If you are not 100% happy with your life today, it is never a waste of time to try something that could get you there.

Fear of Seeming Vain

The third type of fear that stops people from operating in their passion, creating their own opportunities, and attempting to make a meaningful shift in their lives toward financial freedom is the fear of seeming vain. We will get to mindset in the next chapter, but this fear stems from a skewed mindset and perspective. You may think to yourself about just who you are to want something greater out of life. Your parents do not desire greater, and your friends do not desire greater, so why do you think that you deserve better than them? Is it because you think you're better than them? All of these are very real questions that go through people's heads when they think about taking the initiative and trying to chase their dreams. Why do I deserve to be wealthy when everyone else around me is suffering? Is it not disrespectful for those who suffered before you for you to not "pay your dues"?

You deserve to be wealthy because everyone deserves to be wealthy. The ones who take advantage of the opportunities that life presents them with are the ones who make their dreams happen. When I say 'opportunities,' I'm referring to the gifts you were born with, the skills you have, the ability to seek specialized education, and the time to discover your passion. When you take advantage of these, you can then establish a vision that you work towards tirelessly and which will leave a legacy for those who follow. THOSE are opportunities. The same ones that every human on Earth gets, regardless of their race, religion, or creed. The only thing stopping them is their fear, their mindsets, and their lack of conviction.

I have an acronym I use: TAG. God gave everyone talents, abilities, and gifts. You have to shift your perspective to one that thinks like this. Would it not be more disrespectful for you to do absolutely nothing with a gift that God—your creator and the creator of all things—thought so much as to instill in you from birth? When you refuse to use your gifts and walk out your calling, you are not only disrespecting God (as if that's not enough), but you are also disrespecting all the people whose lives you would have touched by not walking out your calling for fear of being vain.

What would've been vain would have been me, LaShawne Holland, choosing not to take on the mantle of "the financial blueprint fixer," "the wealthy lifestyle architect," and "the Queen of Green" (as my clients call me). If I would have done like my guidance counselor told me and picked up a trade because "people like me didn't go to college," I would be letting down each and every person I have ever helped. They might have never had anyone break through to them about creating their own opportunity, cashing in on their passion, developing their business, or establishing wealth systems. Me not walking out my calling would have been vain! That would have been selfish! I would have let down not only my creator but everyone else whose lives I was destined to impact. That is what you need to consider when you are fearful of seeming vain. Your mindset needs to shift so that you can realize all the value you bring to the world, and how selfish it would be for you not to do what you were created to do.

To rein it in on a more practical note, there are a lot of people nowadays who are afraid of the phrase "personal brand." It seems to carry a negative connotation, as though it is pretentious to talk about one's personal brand. I could go on forever about this, but you have to establish a personal brand. Whether you are starting a business, or just working to be the best employee at your dream job at your dream company, everyone has a personal brand. Developing a strong personal brand is key to financial and business success. Do not worry about seeming vain. Embrace it. Embrace your persona; it is who you are. Some people will gravitate toward it, and some won't, but those who genuinely align and agree with how you walk out your calling will become a strong part of your tribe. To some others, this will come off as cocky. They will tear you down. They will ask you who you think you are.

My son Adam raised a good point when he said in one of our conversations that "Nobody is anybody until they are somebody." Oprah wasn't Oprah until she was Oprah. Floyd Mayweather was an illiterate high school dropout before he was Floyd "Money" Mayweather. Do not let them tell you who you are. Rather, in the words of the Black Panther's Mother, "Show them who you are." Finally, do not fear seeming vain. Plenty of people will try and tear you down or accuse you of being pompous for wanting more. The truth is, if you aren't living the life that you visualized at the beginning of this chapter, then you should want more.

You were designed with a destiny in mind, and you should not settle for anything less. So, get ready, because now that we have addressed your fears, it is time for us to work on the single most important thing you need to establish lasting and generational wealth: a wealthy mindset.

Fear is one of the largest hindrances of financial freedom. Millions don't realize that they really have to start investing in themselves at the level that they're currently on. You can't invest for your tomorrow when you're stuck on your today. I wanted to be able to give people the opportunity to start with their personal development and, over time, really increase their financial intelligence so they can make better decisions and lead themselves towards a freedom-based lifestyle.

The predominant concept behind my program, Abundance Attraction Intensive, is about positioning yourself to master your money at your current level so you can invest for your next level. I took the most impressing things that I wish someone would have taught me when I was growing up about money so I could have made better financial decisions and put them in an affordable 12-month program. I believe that it doesn't take courage to say, "I can never achieve anything." Yet that's what our actions show us when we don't pursue the promises of the covenant because of fear. Your actions, your non-focus, says, "I don't really believe. This biblical promise is not really that important to me." When you don't act on the things that you know in your heart belong to you, what you're really saying is, "I don't want to be a blessing to others. I don't desire to build the Kingdom at a greater level." It's essentially telling God, as I've had people tell me, "Well, I don't want to be wealthy." You need to understand that it's not about you. It's not about the money. It's always about the mission. What you're almost saying is, "God, you wasted your time giving me gifts and giving me talents." You're blessed to be a blessing, but you can't be a blessing with an empty cup. You're essentially saying, "I don't want to be an influencer in my generation. I don't really believe 'Thy will be done on Earth as it is in Heaven.'" That's essentially what you're saying when you don't want to become attractive to abundance.

A great way to protect yourself from feeling like a failure is to never try. I deal with a lot people with a poverty mindset who feel this way because things may not have worked out in the past like they thought it should, or because they expected something to work out but they failed completely. That doesn't mean that you're a failure. You just have to look at it differently. Perspective is everything. You have to know how you look at your life. Only you can decide whether you're looking to your potential abundance and wealth from the eyes of a grasshopper or the eyes of a giant.

Fear can be a powerful force. But it only has as much power as you give it. You don't realize that most of the things you fear can ultimately be your strengths if you adopt the right mindset and the right perspective. So, don't fear failure; failure is one of the most essential ingredients to long-term success. Do not fear others' judgment because, at the end of the day, most people aren't thinking about you. Those who don't have anything good to say have opinions that bear no weight on someone making the effort to walk out their calling. Let them watch from the sidelines as you work to better yourself and establish a better financial future for you, your loved ones, and future generations. Even if that someone is yourself, you have to hold steadfast in your vision. Be strong enough to tear down those walls because the walls that protect you from disappointment are the same walls that separate you from your dreams.

It all comes down to your emotional fitness; your psychological strength; your mental agility; your ability to become alive where your money is concerned; and your capacity to be able to take any challenges, difficulties, disappointments, and failures that you experience and convert them into something lasting.

CHAPTER 2

Discover Your Truest "WHY"

I remember this day like it was yesterday. Even though it was 23 years ago, I can still close my eyes and see the room and remember the emotions I was feeling. I was eight months pregnant with my oldest son, Adam, and I was sitting in his nursery one night. I remember looking around at the Noah's-Ark-themed room. As I began to think about his soon-to-be entry into the world, I started thinking about how much I wanted to be able to give him an advantage in life.

I closed my eyes and began to take a trip back down memory lane and thought about how much of a struggle college was for me. I worked three jobs to put myself through college. Even before he was born, I was thinking about his college tuition. I didn't want him to have to struggle like I did. I didn't want him to have to start from ground zero. I wanted to be able to give him the very best education, environment, and experiences.

I started to cry because, at this time, all of these things seemed impossible. I remember making a decision, a resolve, that I would do whatever it took for my ceiling to be his floor. I decided that night that I was going to do whatever it took (legally) to create a different life for him. That night, he became my "WHY." As time went on, and with each child I gave birth to, my "WHY" was enlarged. Life happened, and I discovered my blessing to the Earth, and all the people who needed my guidance became my "WHY." Today, my "WHY" is bigger than anything I could have ever imagined because it includes people in the United States, the Caribbean Islands, Africa, the United Kingdom, Australia, the United

Emirates, India, and Asia. God has truly enlarged my territory and expanded my borders.

Every successful, wealthy, or impactful person in history has always had a "WHY." It is what fuels you. It pushes you through those long nights and forces your eyelids open on those early mornings. Every time you feel like you are about to break, you remind yourself of your "WHY," and you realize that you are not breaking but are bending because your truest "WHY" would never allow you to break. It is not a reach to say that, without a strong "WHY," it is not likely you will be able to continue to reach for your vision as greater and greater obstacles begin to appear. That is why discovering your truest "WHY" is so important.

Most people, when you ask them what their "WHY" is, give a fairly obvious answer. For me, it was my kids. My kids are still my "WHY" and will always continue to be. However, they are not my truest "WHY," although my truest "WHY" is related to them.

A Lot of times, when I'm working with clients in my programs, one of the first topics we deal with is their "WHY." Creating a strong foundation to build upon is paramount. This exercise is so important because building wealth and becoming financially free isn't easy. When things come up and you feel like giving up, your "WHY" becomes your North Star, your guiding light. I want to take you on a journey with me to discovering your TRUEST "WHY."

I discovered my truest "WHY" a few years ago when I first encountered an exercise called Seven Levels Deep. I have come across the exercise a few times in my reading, most recently while reading an amazing book called *Millionaire Success Habits* by Dean Graziosi (a *New York Times* best-seller that I will refer to a couple times in this book and a read I most definitely recommend).

I want to do that exercise now, with you, to help you discover your truest "WHY," the thing that, on the deepest level, will keep you engaged and motivated no matter what obstacle you face because it is that profound and means that much to you. I will walk you through the exercise by taking you through my experience going Seven Levels Deep. I recommend you do this exercise with a friend, spouse, or family member—someone you trust and can feel comfortable letting go with because this exercise digs deep and often gets emotional. You want someone who can respect the passion and value you have for what you're doing and what you aspire to do in the future.

Now, back to the exercise. They call this exercise Seven Levels Deep because you dive progressively deeper into each answer by asking "why" seven times. I want you to begin by asking these questions: Why are you reading this book? Why do you want to be financially free? Why do you want to learn to multiply? Don't pause, and don't stop to think about it; simply let the answers flow naturally. You are with a person you trust, so don't hold back. This needs to be raw.

After you answer, have your partner ask you why. Make sure they repeat your answer as well. If you respond, "Because I don't want to be poor anymore," they need to respond, "Why don't you want to be poor anymore?" Then, with each successive answer, the person doing this exercise with you should repeat each past answer as well as the corresponding "why" questions. Make sure they have a pen and paper ready to take your answers down so they won't forget. To continue this example, once your partner asks why you don't want to be poor anymore, you respond, "Because I have been poor all my life, and I want something different. I need something different." Your partner would then say, "Okay, I asked you why you're reading this book. You told me because you don't want to be poor anymore. I asked you why you don't want to be poor anymore. You said because you have been poor all your life and desire something different. Why do you desire something different?"

It is imperative that you ask "why" seven times. I don't know why seven is the magic number, but it just is. From that initial question of why you are reading this book, you need to go seven *whys* deep. Let it flow. Make sure your answers are natural. Talk through your answers; they don't have to be one sentence long. Think out loud, and you will arrive at the answers for each question just by talking.

Most importantly, do not try to put a wall up before you get emotional. Honesty is crucial. If you have to cry, cry. If it brings you to a painful place from your childhood, you have to go back to that place. This exercise is so powerful is because it gets down to the roots. It shows you why you are who you are and why you want what you want. It's good if it makes you uncomfortable. It's good if you get emotional. These feelings are passion, and they are fuel. These are the same feelings that will light that fire under your butt and help you look whatever obstacles you encounter dead in the face before you move them. It will give you the fire and the passion to move them because you will have a reason to move forward that fires up every bit of essence in your being.

That is what Seven Layers Deep is all about. This will be your weapon against discouragement, exhaustion, and anything else that stands in between you, your vision, and your financial freedom. Once you get to your truest "WHY," I need you to write it down. Word it thoughtfully and specifically. Then, keep it with you. Look at it whenever a family member tells you you're crazy for wanting more, whenever your spouse tells you that you've changed and that you didn't use to work this hard, whenever your boss tells you you're going to fall flat on your face if you go out and try to do something on your own. Your truest "WHY" is stronger than all opposition. It is now your secret weapon. Wield it well on your journey to making your vision a reality.

CHAPTER 3

Mindset, Exposure, & the Stages of Learning

I know what it's like to feel like you're financially suffocating, and I live on the other side of that now. It's really the money mindset shift that caused me to go from making a remedial $40,000 a year to $150,000 a year, and then to make my previous annual income my new monthly income.

The biggest shift in that really was my mindset. My drive, my thoughts, my beliefs, my associations, my habits—all of these things really did have to shift for me. I had to get rid of the internal conflicts that were inside me. Am I worthy of wealth? Am I smart enough? Am I built for the process? Can I become who I need to be in the process? These were all questions that I had to answer for myself. The only limitations that you really have are the belief systems in your head and in your soul, the amount of effort that you put in, and the financial standards that you set for yourself (and that you're going to actually hold yourself to).

The life cycle of poverty, according to society, repeats from generation to generation. I have learned that, even though there are different levels of poverty, the common thread that runs throughout the fabric of scarcity is a poor man's mindset. Middle-class society does not consider itself poor. But this is an illusion.

Now, some may be offended by that statement, so let me get this out of the way early. If you are offended by something I say, GOOD. If the way that I am talking makes you uneasy, GOOD. If something I say makes you uncomfortable, GOOD. Because where has being comfortable gotten you? If you think you are fine with where you are now, wherever that may be, then close this book. I am not here for the people who are fine with where they are. I am here for the people who realize there is something more—something they know is there but which they just can't seem to grasp. I'm talking about those who will never be fine with where they are because success is ongoing. Happiness is solving the problems you love to solve, operating in your passion, and becoming wealthy while you do it. So, you can go take a nap in your little comfort zone, because we were born to MULTIPLY.

Getting back to the idea of middle-class poverty, I can relate, I lived this illusion for a season. I didn't know any better. Everyone I knew was living in the same world. We think because we live in single-family homes that we have somehow arrived, even though we are "house poor" (meaning we can't afford to do much more than pay the mortgage). We can't afford private schools for our children's education in the best school systems, but we can afford a social-media-chronicled vacation. We can't afford to put money away for retirement or life insurance, but the payments look completely manageable for a new Mercedes.

The middle class focuses on creating the illusion of wealth, instead of creating wealth systems. We are obsessed with dressing like we sit at the table while settling for crumbs, instead of building a chair to reach the table. Better yet, we should strive to own the chair, the table, the building the table is in, and the air space above it. We often choose not to build the chair even though that chair could be used to seat not only us but generations that come after us if only we take the time to build a sturdy foundation.

Now, I don't know of any chairs built from passive income and wealth systems, but hopefully, you get the idea. It is all about mindset. The subconscious poverty mentality plaguing the middle class undergirds our drive to prop up the upper-class illusion.

> **You have to work hard for an illusion. You have to work smart for a legacy.**

What you are leaving now is a legacy of debt.

It is a legacy of living paycheck to paycheck. We're not buying assets;

we're buying liabilities that we think are assets. They're not assets because true assets put money in your pocket and food on the table. Liabilities take money out of your pocket, and they don't put food on the table. That is the simplest way to explain the difference between an asset and a liability. We've just been deceived into thinking that, for middle-class America, wealth is defined by the car you drive or the purse you sport, not even realizing that the middle class is the highest-taxed pawn in the game of money.

The roads that are built, the bridges that are constructed, all of this is built off the backs of middle-class America because we haven't educated ourselves on how to shift tax brackets or money quadrants. There is a phenomenon I talk about a lot called the Six Figure Deceiver. Many people in today's world think that once they have a six-figure salary, they've "made it." This is a deceiving mindset because even though, by your standards, you seem "rich" on paper, you're still struggling to get ahead like everyone else. Six figures does not mean the same thing now that it did in the '80s. That is because of a little thing I like to call inflation. Three invisible hands are always in people's wallets: inflation, taxes, and debt. You cannot control inflation or taxes. But you can control your debt. If you had $100,000 in salary in 1980, that is the equivalent of $288,713 right now—even more by the time you are reading this. To rephrase, a person would need to make almost $300,000 today to afford the same lifestyle as someone who made $100,000 in 1980. That is why inflation is one of the major invisible hands in the Six Figure Deceiver. $100,000 just isn't what it used to be.

We haven't even gotten to taxes yet. People don't realize that for the first six months of the year, you are working just to pay taxes. When you look at the setup of our current tax structure, the middle class and those six-figure earners are getting taxed the most. Nearly half of what you make goes to Uncle Sam. If you're not a business owner, taxes are one of your largest expenses. Many people don't realize it, but the Internal Revenue Tax Codes were written to favor the wealthy, not the middle class or the poor. Two hours of every single day you spend working is done to feed our government. People don't realize that 25%-35% of your life is spent paying taxes.

If you aren't interested in learning how to minimize your taxes, you should be. One of the things my tax accountant professor taught me years ago is that inflation eats away at the spending power of our dollar and it also places us into higher tax brackets. Taxes steal your money, your time, and your future financial growth opportunities. So, when you look at how much of your income you lose in taxes if you make $100,000, then you are looking to get out of debt and move forward with $50,000. That is really what you are bringing home, and people don't see that—I call it 50% money. They are readily deceived by this outdated mindset that once you make six figures, you are living the good life and deserve to splurge. I am not knocking your hard work. There are plenty of people who go their whole lives not making six figures. Just know that you haven't made it, and you need to keep going. That same diligence and work it took you to get there, you will need to double—no, triple—down on it to make it to the next level. So, do not be deceived by this fake wealth benchmark. We will define what true wealth is in the next chapter; just you wait.

We have to learn how to make these institutions work for us. I often tell people that CASHFLOW is the most important financial term in the world of money. Money in the market is never lost. Cash is always flowing. ALWAYS. That is why they call it currency. It's always flowing in or flowing out. For 98% of households, it flows out. True financial freedom means that cash flows TO YOU and not AWAY FROM YOU. Knowing which direction your cash is flowing is paramount if you want your money to multiply and build wealth. I had to learn what true wealth is and how to govern it. I had to learn how to become a money master, not just a money manager. People often look for that one thing that will make them wealthy, but it's not just one thing. It's a collage of things that work in synergy, and you have to be committed to learning what the rules are in the game of money and wealth. You have to define wealth for yourself. The starting point is to stop letting the entertainment industry, athletes, and social media posts define what wealth looks like to you.

Really, 80% of success in anything—80% of wealth—is psychological. It's your mindset, your ability to take whatever life has thrown at you and convert it into a new set of actions, a new set of habits, a new set of belief systems, a new set of ideas, a new set of insights that finally gets you to where you want to be. In order for you to do that, you often have to ask people, "Who is the person that you need to be to become abundance-attractive?"

20% of financial success rests in money mechanics—things like spending plans, written visions, etc.

I remember a couple of decades ago when I read a series of books that totally changed my life and my mindset about money. But it was one book in particular by Robert Kiyosaki called *Cashflow Quadrant* that skyrocketed my corporate ladder climb. The book is based on four quadrants: Employee, Self-Employed, Business Owner, and Investor. The people on the left side of the quadrant (employees and the self-employed) pay the most money in taxes. The people on the right side of the quadrant (business owners and investors) pay the least in taxes. The people on the right side of the quadrant live in a completely different world than those on the left. It was then that I realized it's expensive to be poor in America.

One day, I was reading the Bible, and I **SAW** the Cashflow Quadrant® that Robert Kiyosaki was talking about. I wanted to scream. Jesus's disciples were out on the water all night and had just returned to the shore. "Go back out into deeper waters," Jesus told them (I'm paraphrasing). "Look, Jesus, we've been out all night long and we haven't caught anything. Our nets are empty," they replied. To that, Jesus said, "I want you to go back. But not only back into deeper waters. I want you to go into deeper waters and to cast your net on the RIGHT SIDE of the boat." Jesus could have told them to just put their nets out there, but he didn't. He said, "cast it on the RIGHT SIDE of the boat." It was then that I had an *aha* moment that hit me like a ton of bricks. It became clear to me that what I had been reading in Cashflow Quadrant® was a biblical principle AND a wealth building principle.

Jesus was talking about left-side cashflow versus right-side cashflow. So, when we look at the Cashflow Quadrant®, we dismantle the financial illusion by creating business systems and investing—that is, by operating on the right side of the quadrant. No one teaches us how to use our talents, our abilities, and our gifts to create revenue rivers. (I don't want to say just "income streams"; I want rivers, not multiple streams of income. Streams dry up easily. Rivers flow for centuries.)

We must learn not only what true wealth is, but we must also learn the strategies that keep us wealthy. Part of building and maintaining wealth is understanding taxes. The same tax codes that are currently the bane of your existence can also allow you to keep more of what you have earned in your possession. I'm not talking about tax evasion—that's a crime—but I am talking about legal ways to reduce your tax liability because I don't want to have to pay more than my fair share. We bash people who take the time to learn the tax codes and choose to leverage them to their advantage. We would rather remain complacent and victimized than position ourselves to no longer be the victim. Part of the equation of wealth building is learning how to use the tax code to keep more money. The government rewards us when we use the tax code. Those who create jobs, housing, and opportunities are subsidized. They don't reward you for having earned income. Only your boss does that. He or she wants you to keep being a great employee so they can give you a fat bonus to be taxed at 45% while they get to write off the expense of paying your bonus so they can lessen their tax liability. Brilliant, isn't it?

The wealthy are concerned with financial security while they have money. In the African American community, we are only concerned with financial security once the money has left our hands, once it's too late. This is where the idea of exposure comes in. Mindset and exposure go hand-in-hand. What you are exposed to shapes your mindset. That is all you know, and you can't be blamed for that. It is the environment you were raised in. That is why I worked so hard to send my children to independent, college prep schools so they could see what true wealth looks like, learn about wealth practices, and see how wealth whispers. This way, they could also see through the "faux wealth" that they were exposed to in the media by rappers and ballplayers. Growing up, the majority of what we know about being "rich" is learned from popular media because that is all we are exposed to. I made sure that my children, from an early age, knew the difference between being "rich" and being wealthy. Now, while you are not responsible for what you were exposed to as a child, you are responsible for what you continue to expose yourself to as an adult.

The Four Stages of Learning

Life is a journey. That journey can be hard and painstaking, or it can be relatively smooth and fulfilling. No route is free of hills or potholes. But some are a lot more efficient and exponentially more rewarding than others. In psychology, there is something called the Four Stages of Competence, also known as the Four Stages of Learning. Stage 1 is Unconscious Incompetence. The learner is not even aware that a knowledge or skill gap exists. The blinders are on, and they are blissfully ignorant of the possibilities available to them. They continue down the road they're on because, according to what they know, it is the only road available.

Stage 2 is Conscious Incompetence. This is the stage in which learning can begin. In this stage, the learner becomes consciously aware of a knowledge or skill disparity. This occurs through exposure. In real life, exposure occurs when you put in the effort to put something different into your eye gate. The most immediate, effective, and greatly underrated way someone can increase their exposure is, of course, through reading. After you expose yourself to the practices, lessons, and mindsets of the wealthy, you become painfully aware of the disparity between the way you think and the way those who aspire to leave generational wealth think. Now, the blinders are off. The learner looks around and is shocked to discover that there are hundreds—no, thousands—of other routes they could be taking.

They continue to read. They go to conferences and listen to podcasts covering a variety of industries. From every one of these books, events, and sources, they pick up more puzzle pieces. Some of the pieces aren't useful for the puzzle they are trying to build, but some are. They see the way the pieces begin to fit together. Then, when they put together the right ones, they begin to see the final picture form.

You could do the same. Maybe you read Robert Kiyosaki and decided you want to pursue real estate. He revealed to you the ways of accruing tax-free wealth through real estate investment and the art of leveraging debt and OPM (other people's money) to do so. You looked up and said to yourself, "That's what I want to do!" Or maybe you read Robert Kiyosaki and decided that you eventually want to get involved in real estate, but you also realize that you don't currently have the money to do so. Do you rush to take out a loan you cannot afford? Do you give up, take the easy way out, and write it off as something only rich people who already have money can do? Or do you continue to educate yourself and continue to read a spectrum of books about the wealthy and their practices?

Let's say you choose the latter and come across the writings of Peter Schiff, an investing expert and powerhouse in the field. You resolve that you will take the little money you have and learn how to effectively invest that in the market. Then, once your sum has grown through market investments, you will take it out of the market and use it to invest in real estate. Are you seeing the stars align? Do you see the puzzle begin to come together? Purchasing six-figure properties that could cost a lifetime to afford seemed out of reach, but now that you have a plan and reasonable means to afford these properties within the next 5-10 years, it doesn't seem impossible.

Now, this is just an example, but a completely realistic one, nonetheless. Exposing yourself to more information allows you to uncover the hidden paths that are available to you. The learner becomes aware of the different paths he or she can take along his or her journey, spending time on certain routes before crossing over to others. The learner creates their own unique path by using the roadmaps and following the routes that have already been charted by others who have been successful on the journey.

This brings us to Stage 3. The third stage is Conscious Competence. In this stage, the learner is knowledgeable and aware enough to know how to use the skill or perform the task in question. However, doing so requires conscious effort, thought, and hard work. After becoming knowledgeable and aware of the different routes available, the learner chooses the route that their natural talents lend them to and which their current resources allow them to. Then, the learner completely devotes him or herself to plotting this course in a way that is targeted, efficient, and methodical.

Being in this stage means that you listened to podcasts on blockchain technology, you took a course on ecommerce and dropshipping, and you went to a conference on social media influencing. But, to stick with our example, now that you have decided on stock market investing and eventually real estate, you devote yourself exclusively to those ventures. Think of it like deciding on a college major. Through your studies, you take notes, adhere to guidelines, and use them to avoid any holes in the road along the path that you've chosen. However, you are not an expert. The learner must still look down and refer to their roadmap, their notes, frequently. Of course, they will trip and fall along the way. Knowledge can only do so much—experience is the greatest teacher.

But, after a while, the learner will have looked at that map so many times that they have memorized it. The learner no longer has to check for potholes because they unconsciously jump over them, eyes forward with a never-wavering gaze. Before, the learner couldn't move very quickly. They had to keep looking down to check the map. Now, the learner knows the route. Like an experienced hurdler, the learner now never looks at the hurdles in front of them. The learner's eyes are locked on the finish line as muscle memory takes over and they unconsciously overcomes their obstacles.

This is the last stage: Unconscious Competence. The learner has enough experience with the skill that they can perform it unconsciously. When you've achieved this stage, you don't have to refer to your notes when you are contemplating buying a stock. You analyze it quickly, make your decision, and before you know it, you're on to the next one. You, as the learner, are now sprinting along that path. The journey of life and the route you have chosen to your destiny become a lot smoother when you have the ultimate tool to help you avoid all the potholes and blowouts that make life hell for so many people around us: knowledge.

Please do not misunderstand me—education never ends. The wealthiest people in the world still attend masterminds, read books, and attend conferences because they know the world is constantly changing. As soon as you stop moving forward, you get left behind. Humble yourself. Realize that you are a student in a lesson that will never end, no matter how wealthy you become. Combine this with the lesson we learned earlier. The wealthiest people are those who provide the most value and who do the most good for as many people as they can. Remember Oprah? Tony Robbins?

This unrelenting pursuit of knowledge combined with an uncompromising desire to provide the most value you can to as many people as possible will allow you to accrue enough wealth as a BY-PRODUCT to last your family for generations. Are you starting to see the differences in the priorities and mindsets between the poor, the "rich," and the wealthy? If you are truly focused on the right things, everything else you want will naturally fall in line. It all begins with exposure and mindset.

Now that you are reading this book, you are becoming consciously aware that your idea of prosperity is probably distorted. It is your job to remedy that. In order to be wealthy, you have to think wealthy, and the wealthy flush their thoughts out where those with the drive to discover them will go looking: books and specialized education.

Most of us see money only as a means for acquiring goods and paying bills. But money has so many more functions, especially making you more money. In fact, that is the primary function of the tool called money. A producer multiplies. I learned this while reading the Bible, and it stuck out to me as clear as day. It is there in plain writing, in Matthew 25:14-30, that we were created to multiply. But the world has taught us how to be "money managers." I hate that term almost as much as I hate the term "budget." We weren't created to live inside a budget. You cannot get out of debt by means of a budget. You get out of debt by expanding your means. Years ago, when my family was in debt, Rob and I did exactly that.

Not only were we created to multiply, but the Lord rewards us for doing so. He rewards us for being producers. Not only that, but he punishes those who do not use their gifts and multiply. I remember when I first had this revelation. It was after I read Matthew 25:14-30.

These verses tell the story of a master who was going on a journey and left bags of money with each of his servants. He told them to take care of his things while he was gone and decided how much each servant would be able to care for. He gave one five "talents" (bags) of money. He gave another servant two bags. He gave the last servant one bag. The servant who was given five bags of money quickly went and invested it. By investing those bags of money, he made five more. The servant who was given two bags also invested his money and earned two more. But the last servant went to a secluded place, dug a hole, and hid the master's money underground. When the master returned, he asked his good and faithful servants what they had done with his money. The first servant brought forth ten bags to the master and told the master that he trusted him to take care of five bags of money, so he used them to earn five more. The master responded that he was a good and trustworthy servant who did well with that small amount of money. As a result, the master promised him he would trust him to take care of greater things in the future. The second servant went and fetched his four bags, telling the master that he used the two bags of money to earn two more. The master told him he was a good servant who could be trusted. He did well with a small amount of money, so the master would let him care for much greater things in the future. The last servant went and dug up the one bag of money the master had given to him and brought it back. He told the master that he knew the master was a hard man, a man who was serious about his money and his investments and collecting interest from his money. Therefore, he was afraid of the master and of losing his money, so he simply buried it. The master yelled at the servant, calling him a bad and lazy servant. He asked this servant why, if he knew that the master liked investing his money and reaping interest, he didn't invest the money or at least put it in the bank so it could earn interest. The master then commanded his other servants to take the one bag of money the master had given this servant and give it to the man who had invested the five bags to get ten. "Everyone who uses what they have will get more," the master told them. "They will have much more than they need, but people who do not use what they have will have everything taken away from them. Throw that useless servant outside into the darkness."

There are a couple of lessons to learn from this. The first that I noticed is that the master did not explicitly tell the servants to multiply what he gave them. He simply told them to "take care" of his belongings. How could the third servant know what he meant by that? It made me think that his treatment of the third servant might have been a little too harsh. I mean, how are you going to be so hard on someone who you did not give directions to and who is literally a servant? His whole job entails taking directions.

However, this is all another indicator of mindset. See, for a wealthy person, to take care of their talents and money IS to invest it. For the wealthy, if you hand them a sizeable chunk of money, they are more than likely going to put it in the market, invest it in a business, or invest it in themselves via specialized education from a coach or mastermind. They understand that this is the most logical course of action because money is not just a means to acquire goods (as those with a poor mindset see it). Money is a tool to be leveraged and multiplied to acquire assets or skills that can be put toward establishing generational wealth systems. Money is a way to freedom; it is the seed that you plant in the right place so that a plant will grow that feeds you for the rest of your life. Someone with a poor mindset will receive money and simply squander it. They will purchase a liability or stash their money away if someone told them to "take care" of it. They would take care of it, alright—take care all the way down to the Maserati dealership.

So, how did the first two servants know what to do while the third didn't? The first two servants had vision. They did not intend on being servants forever. The third servant only knew to do what he was told, as is a servant's only job. But, just as in real life, in this parable, it was those that looked beyond their job to what they were destined to be that ended up succeeding.

If you know you're destined to own your own business but are still working a 9-5 somewhere, you need to shift your thinking from that of an employee to that of a business owner, just like these servants shifted their thinking from being mindless servants to being investing masters. You have to paint a clear vision of what you want your future to look like. The third servant saw himself as a servant who could never be anything more, while the first two had a vision for themselves and were already looking for ways to make their reality match that vision.

Even for those of you who do not plan on owning your own business and who, instead, are passionate about being the best employee you can be, you should be thinking like your boss. That way, you are always looking to go beyond whatever your specific job is and are looking to provide more value to the company. The more value you provide, the less dispensable you become. However, it is normally the bosses who are concerned with adding value to the company and furthering its overall mission. The first two servants did not know that their master would allow them to keep the bags of money, but they acted as if he would, and so they took actions to increase its value despite it not being theirs. That is what a great employee does. They work for a company as if it was theirs. They think outside of the box, outside of their job description, and create a better business system for those around them. The bottom line is, whether you are aiming to be an employer or simply the best employee you can be,

> **you have to have a mindset that steers you to act appropriately when life presents you with an opportunity to turn your vision into your reality.**

As a point that piggybacks the reason that the first two servants did not need to be told to invest their bags, those with a wealthy mindset learn from those who are already successful. They understand that successful people leave clues for the rest of us. So often, especially in entrepreneurship, people think that they are doing this all on their own and that there is no playbook. Chances are, whatever you are doing, someone has done it (or at least something similar to it) and has been successful at it. Research that person, see how they did things, and emulate them. You do not have to reinvent the wheel when someone has already laid out a blueprint. You just have to take the initiative to do what they do. That is why these two servants immediately emulated the master. They saw that he was successful—heck, they were HIS servants. If what the master did with his money brought him so much wealth and prosperity, why would they do anything different? For them, it was a no-brainer. That is why they didn't need to be told what to do with their bags of money. They had observed success in motion and followed the blueprint. Copying successful people, and thereby saving time and money, is at the heart of a wealthy mindset.

The last servant ignored the practices that the master taught through action. He was scared and was looking for someone to show him how to do it, or he would simply do nothing at all. You cannot get into the wrong mindset and think you are all alone, as if you are the first person who has ever started a business. That is how new entrepreneurs remain paralyzed with fear. Every business owner and every wealthy person had to start somewhere, and, like I said, their success leaves clues. Those with a wealthy mindset follow them, and it saves them plenty of time, money, and headaches.

Another key point is that the first two servants were poised to take advantage of the situation. They had the education and the wherewithal so that when they finally were presented with an opportunity, they knew what to do to take advantage of it. There is a whole chapter later in this book related to opportunity recognition, so I will not go too deep into that just yet. But you need to be prepared in advance when an opportunity presents itself, and this kind of preparation is a hallmark characteristic of someone with a wealthy mindset. You wouldn't wait until the coach puts you in the game to start practicing three-pointers. You would have already spent hours on end shooting in the gym, studying, learning, and taking the initiative. You should practice like a starter even though you may never get the opportunity to play in the game. That is all a part of mindset and vision.

The same goes for your wealth. When you have a vision for yourself and you know where you are destined to be, you need to prepare yourself in advance for when an opportunity comes that can help you make your vision a reality. I was reading *Robb Report*, *Worth*, and *Forbes Magazine* long before I could afford to read anything other than *Ebony*. I visualized what it would be like before I got there so that I would be prepared. I would not be fearful like the third servant. I would know what to do when I acquired the wealth I was destined for because my mindset, vision, and preparation via self-investment and education would shine through any doubt in my heart.

This is the mindset you must always have because you never know what type of opportunity will present itself or when it will present itself. You could find yourself in a Waffle House with Mark Cuban late one night after a Mavs game. He runs in to use the bathroom. You have till the time he is done doing the deed, and hopefully washing his hands, and comes out to leave to devise your next move. Someone with a wealthy mindset would have been preparing for a moment like this for their whole lives. They have their number memorized, they have watched elevator-pitch-tip videos and read books on how to make the perfect pitch. They competed in pitch competitions to adjust their nerves to the spotlight. They have developed their business acumen by attending mastermind groups, business development conferences, and reading books like this one. They take that opportunity, and they multiply it. Next thing you know, they're standing on the set of *Shark Tank*, poised to make a deal with one or multiple astute investors, with millions of potential customers watching. This is the breakthrough they've been waiting for, but it only came about because they already had the mindset of an entrepreneur and were ready to persuade and do business with the best of the best and make their "talents" multiply.

One of the last major points that I took away from this story is the master's promise that the servants would now be trusted with more since they had proven that they were competent with less. Many people sit around and complain that they just haven't gotten their big break yet, but what have such people done with the opportunities they have been given? Those with a wealthy mindset look to maximize whatever opportunity that can help them achieve their goals and further their vision.

Maybe you are an entrepreneur who owns their own cupcake company.

You try to gear yourself toward large events like weddings, corporate events, or catered galas, but the only events you have been able to book lately are small birthday parties or family gatherings. You rack your brain as to why your vision isn't happening for you. However, you show up late to every one of your events. Your presentation is sloppy. You are not well-dressed. You don't attempt to form relationships and establish new customer leads. Beyonce's party planner could be in attendance at one of these events, just looking for someone to cater Blue Ivy's birthday party, and you would be none the wiser. The universe, God, whatever you believe in, will not present a person with new opportunities if they have done nothing with the ones they are given.

Later on, I devote an entire chapter to opportunity recognition, but this concept goes hand-in-hand with mindset. You are not above anything that has the potential to further your vision. You should show up to every one of those small events dressed like you were servicing the Obamas. You should meet and connect with the guests. You should have an extraordinary setup because you will never get a second chance to make a first impression. You will begin to attract that which you emit. You will find yourself servicing more large-scale and upper-echelon events because that is the image you are evoking and the energy you are putting into the universe. It is all about walking out your vision long before you are put in a place that begins to look like that vision. When you show that you know what to do with a little and that you can multiply what is in your hands now, I guarantee you that you will begin to attract whatever you truly desire. Even if you are barely surviving, you have to conduct business like you are thriving.

Speaking of surviving versus thriving, there's a difference in your grind when you're pursuing freedom instead of mere survival. That, as well, comes down to a difference in mindset. I remember that when my children were young, I would take them through gated communities and point to the mansions while telling them, "Those are employers, not employees." Employers chase freedom. They wish for the ability to take time off whenever they want. They aspire to have the freedom to retire whenever it is needed. They aspire to have the freedom to be able to help whatever charitable cause is nearest to their heart. They want the freedom to touch as many people as possible with their gift, regardless of whether they'll profit from it. They desire the freedom to die without worrying about whether the generations they leave behind will be able to eat. Employers—and, by extension, the wealthy—pursue freedom.

Employees, the middle class, and the lower class pursue survival. They are not concerned with putting food on the next generation's table because theirs is still empty. They are so concerned with keeping up with the Joneses that when a real financial or market crisis comes along, they are one step removed from homelessness. They cannot afford to plan for tomorrow because they are still trying to see if they can afford today.

You have to be able to lift your head high enough to see the possibilities. Work to give yourself the breathing room necessary to finally be able to look beyond tomorrow, beyond this year, beyond your lifetime. Your horizon is so short when you have a narrow mindset. People like Warren Buffett aren't interested in tomorrow, or even next year. They sit on a level where the only time frame relevant to them is the next 60 years. That is why current investors in the market can only hope to ride on their coattails. Those big players and the firms they control make the market because they have the freedom and resources to do so.

Those who grind with the aim of attaining freedom are the ones who constantly invest in themselves. They know that the world is always changing and that they need to constantly educate themselves if they expect to remain prepared for it. The average person will look at their life right now and decide that because they are "okay" today (that term being relative), they do not need to worry about tomorrow. A person with a wealthy mindset realizes that there is no time for complacency. We have to evolve constantly, just as the world around us does. To refer back to Stage 2 of the Stages of Learning I discussed earlier, those with a wealthy mindset are aware that there will always be a disparity between what they know and the new dynamic they face DAILY as an unquantifiable number of domestic and international forces—from all different sectors, from politics to nanotechnology—constantly interact to form a completely new global landscape.

Before I move on to vision, I want to address one more major mindset flaw that people in the lower and middle classes have about the wealthy: the misconception that one cannot be both happy and wealthy, that in order to have one, you must sacrifice the other. That is a scarcity mindset. Essentially, you are budgeting your life. You are limiting your life by saying that in order to have one thing you have to give up another. That is simply not true. The poor look for ways to conserve what they have, while the wealthy look for ways to acquire more. If you cannot accommodate both happiness and wealth into your current lifestyle, then it is time for you to upgrade your lifestyle.

See, people have a misconception that happiness is a place, a destination that you suddenly arrive at in life where you look around and just feel fulfilled. It's a problem-free environment, where you don't have a care in the world, where you lay down in the grass, the screen fades to black, and the crowd gives a standing ovation.

However, happiness is not the absence of problems. So many of us go through life trying to avoid every problem or inconvenience. I'm going to break some news to you: Life is an endless series of problems that are meant to be solved. God gave you His power so that you can solve problems. The solution to one problem is merely the creation of another. Do not hope for a life without problems. There is no such thing. Instead, hope for a life full of **GOOD** problems, of problems that you enjoy solving. It is the challenge that makes it all worth it.

Think about the best moments in your life. They all came after you accomplished something that shocked you, something that was not easy but which, upon completion, made you feel like you could do anything. The truth is, all things are possible for those who believe. Believe what? That you have been given the ability to be a problem-solver.

However, solving problems and accomplishing feats in areas you have no passion for will leave you feeling unfulfilled in the long run. You need to figure out what problems you enjoy solving. That is your passion. Start a business in line with that. Find a career in that field.

Who you are is defined by what you are willing to sacrifice for.

To be happy, we need something to solve. Happiness is therefore a form of action. It is not a mountaintop that you reach. It is not a certain level of wealth. It is not a destination. Happiness is achieved through constant motion. That is why wealthy people always want more. That is why they never stop moving forward: because one's comfort zone is not only the enemy of progress; it is the enemy of true happiness.

My goal is to get you to a place where you're truly financially free. First, though, you have to change your money mindset. You can't become a master investor without first investing in yourself. You can't be attracted to wealth and abundance with a poverty mindset. It doesn't work. It's like oil and water—the two just don't mix. You can't become a master of your money if you're constantly spending all you have. None of these things are wealth strategies. However, resetting your mindset will not only allow you to make money, but it will also allow you to multiply it and enjoy it.

Wealth attracts wealth, just like abundance attracts abundance. When you have a wealthy mindset, you make different decisions than when you're struggling. You stop pretending, and you start really prospering. Most people aren't ready for wealth. They think they are, but they're not. A wealthy mindset guides you to the kinds of things that expand you instead of shrink you. When you start looking at the habits, beliefs, and actions of people who are truly wealthy, you understand that their decision-making process really is different than that of people who aren't wealthy. When you feel like your life is lacking something, you hold back and you look at the world very differently. You don't make the same types of decisions that you would if your financial situation were to change.

If you really want to attack your finances and you really want to live a freedom-based lifestyle and become financially free, you have to look at your situation from three points.

1. Your mindset (or, as I call it, your money psychology). Like I said earlier, 80% of success in anything is in the way you think. If you really want to go deep into this, I have a program called Money Mindset Mastery, where we actually walk you through the steps. Spending all you have without having a surplus at the end of the month is not a wealth strategy. People who have poor financial habits really do have a poverty mindset. The Bible talks about how a fool spends all that he has. We have to look at that, at how we're thinking. What's the psychology behind it? If we're successful in shifting that, we position ourselves for abundance.

2. We have to look at the mechanics. Ask yourself: What formulas and strategies really work? What's the core element of the things that I really need to do to attain total financial freedom? Just because you don't have any credit card debt does not mean that you are living a financially free lifestyle. Wealth is measured in time, not in dollars. If you don't have the

time to, for instance, spend 60 days on the beaches of Bora Bora without worrying about your money, then you're not financially free. Financial freedom, financial independence, and financial security are measured in time.

We have to take the time to look at these things. Are you going to be in a position to have all the money you want and need so you don't have to work for the rest of your life? Money to do what you want? Money to go where you want? Money to live how you want to? Can you get to the point where working is no longer a requirement for you and you can honestly say, "I work because I want to, not because I have to"? It's about you living a life of significance.

3. What do you do to make sure that you keep it? It really is about being able to make it, to multiply it, and then retain it for future generations. We have to become generationally minded. I often tell those who I teach about one of the things that my grandfather used to tell me growing up all the time: "LaShawne, what you do in moderation, your kids will grow up to do in excess." We look at the amount of debt that Americans have today. We look at the scarcity that people live in and the percentage of people who live in poverty. The gap between the haves and the have-nots in the United States is getting larger and larger and larger. There is a sector of people who will build a fortune, multiply it, and leave it for their children, but statistics show that it takes only three generations to lose your money again. That's why being able to master your money mindset is so important.

Consumer v. Producer

I started teaching my kids the concept of consumer versus producer very early on. When they started elementary school, Rob and I began to have small conversations with them about what defines a producer and what defines a consumer, as well as how to identify both. Producers are those who make their own food, create their own wealth, invest, and create business systems. They do not rely on someone else to feed them. They create their own economic opportunities. A consumer depends on another to provide them with their opportunities, their options as to what they do with their money, and whether or not food gets put on their table.

I remember when Adam was in the 5th or 6th grade, and he wanted a really expensive pair of Jordans. They were $380, to be exact. I remember standing in the shoe store having the conversation how he was Michael Jordan's asset and how Michael Jordan was his liability. I remember saying, "I am not spending this much on tennis shoes that cost $7.00 to produce." (I was part-owner of a company that was doing overseas manufacturing at the time, so I knew the deal.) Ultimately, I did not deny him the Jordans, but I did make him purchase stock in Nike with his birthday money. I made sure he knew that in that current consumer structure, he was Michael Jordan's asset, and MJ was his liability.

Now, I don't intend to offend anyone reading this book. I never do, but it happens. A lot of times when you get angry or defensive, it's just because you were forced to examine or question an aspect of your life you were secure about, and now someone is suggesting that you re-evaluate that security. I am not asking you not to have feelings; I am only asking you to acknowledge those feelings and to then be receptive to what I have to say because I think it can really help you in the long run.

Getting back to the idea of consumers versus producers. Consumers are those with plantation mindsets. We can only eat what is fed to us, and we can only work in certain capacities, while others dictate what we spend our money on. We need to recognize that the average 21st-century consumer is simply a 21st-century slave. You only eat if the master feeds you (i.e., if your employer pays you). But you don't know how to cook. If you stepped out on your own, you would not have the knowledge to be able to feed yourself. This is why knowledge is so important to creating your own opportunities.

As a 21st-century slave, you go to school, pick from a handful of jobs that fall in line with the system. Then you get to work, put money in your 401k, and don't worry about your future or retirement because someone is telling you it will work out. We buy what is thrust into our faces, even when these things actually do nothing to further our financial futures. This is bondage, and producers are those who break those bonds and move freely to make their own choices, provide for themselves, and do not depend on the system for opportunities.

A good illustration of consumers versus producers is playing out right now with this 2019 government shutdown. Due to circumstances that are completely out of the normal American's control, hundreds of thousands of people have now gone almost a month without being paid, and who knows how much longer they will have to hold out? In my family growing up, the most successful of us were the ones who got a good government job with a nice pension plan and a yearly cost-of-living raise. I am not knocking government jobs—there are plenty out there that pay great money and are secure—but at the end of the day, you are still at the mercy of an entity that you have no control over. With the current president in office, no one has much control over him.

Now, this holds true for pretty much all jobs, not just government jobs. A sudden shift in tides and demands can make or break companies. Think about all of the people who worked for Blockbuster. They had no idea that a turn of events that took place in the span of just over a decade would leave them out of a job after working for a multi-billion-dollar company. The key is to acquire and hone skills that can be applied in a variety of ways that many companies have a need for.

I am not against people having jobs. I am against jobs having people, meaning that if anything shifts at the company, the person's standard of living is interrupted. For example, someone working at Blockbuster could've been very skilled at product positioning. They were handy with algorithms and data that analyzed the best order in which to display movies on the shelves to grab people's attention. When Blockbuster shut down, he could have easily gone to work for Netflix and apply his skills in a digital landscape to provide information on how to best arrange their catalogs, new movie suggestions, etc.

The key idea here is that producers create their own opportunities by making their talents indispensable. The most obvious instance of a producer is one who starts their own company. They put food on other people's tables; they establish wealth systems. But not everyone is meant to be an entrepreneur; if you're not, you can still create high-value employment opportunities for yourself if you make yourself indispensable. I have friends with amazing compensation packages (like millions in annual salary) because they bring high utility to the companies they work for.

There are numerous aspects of your life that you can implement or cut out in order to be a producer. For example, you could start investing. A consumer puts their money in a 401k or lets someone else manage it who bears no consequence if they lose all they own. If you educate yourself about how to invest, you can create your own opportunities, your own cashflow, and your own means of putting money on the table, even if you work for somebody else. If you are a government worker who has been out of work for a month due to a shutdown but you have experience and education in day trading, you can take whatever little you might have saved up, put that in the stock market, and keep you and your family afloat. You see, producers are resourceful and knowledgeable. They will have food on the table regardless of whether it is served to them or they cook it themselves. This is because producers have vision. They have a clearly-thought-out picture of what they want in life, and every move they make is a step toward that.

Vision

I know I have mentioned it a number of times before, but now I really want to delve into the idea of vision. It is a critical component of a wealthy mindset. It's important to remember that everything you see in the physical started off in the non-physical. From the wheel to the rocket, everything starts out as a vision. They were ideas inside of a person's head—ideas that, with determination, education, goal-setting, and time, eventually manifested in reality.

I just mentioned how many do not lift their heads high enough to see opportunity. In both the literal and figurative sense, you have to have vision. Having vision is what allows the wealthy to see money as something more than just a means of survival. As a result of vision, wealthy people and poor or middle-class people see everything—time, education, language, even meals—completely differently. Poor people like quantity because they have been programmed to have a survival mindset. The more they can have, the more they can fill up on and keep because, subconsciously, they realize that their next meal isn't guaranteed. This is also why poor people do not like upscale restaurants. They prefer quantity over quality. A wealthy person can appreciate the art that goes into a beautifully prepared meal, savor the experience, and leave knowing that they do not have to be full because they know they will eat again.

One of my friends who is big in the health and wellness industry always tells me how you are not supposed to eat until you are full. Those who are only focused on survival, however, succumb to their basic instinct and do eat until they're full. We are only exposed to money as a tool of survival because we were raised in a survivalist landscape. Most of us grew up focusing on ends meeting, and nothing more, because ends meeting was hard enough. So, that is still our horizon as adults because we lack vision. You can only envision what you have been exposed to and what you have seen.

That's why I paid for my children to go to schools where they could see what life was like inside the white picket fence while Rob and I were still working to get there. We wanted them to know what we were working towards and sacrificing for so they would have visions of their own and could meet us in stride when they were old enough to walk beside us in our dreams.

When you have vision, like aspirations of touching the masses, leaving a legacy, or having your name in the history books, you realize that money is a means to much more than just clothes on your back and food on the table. Money is a tool that allows you to have options; it allows you to realize your destiny and leave a legacy that impacts many more people than just yourself. Money gives you reach; in order to reach, you must be free. You cannot be bound by the bills you have today. You cannot be stifled by short-term barricades to your breakthroughs. You will never truly succeed unless your vision is bigger than your obstacles.

> **You will never truly succeed unless your vision is bigger than your obstacles.**

That is what fuels you to extend your horizon and look beyond your bills and your debt. My vision afforded me the nerve to take that Christmas bonus and use it to make an investment rather than pay off bills or spend it. My vision is what empowered me to see my progression and take that next step from vending machines into real estate. My vision is what fueled me to know that I could become knowledgeable enough about real estate to make enough money with it to completely wipe out my debt (and then some) and eventually purchase a brokerage firm.

Those obstacles are certainly daunting, but when you have a vision that is even greater, all of the bills, debt, and long nights are microscopic in comparison. Once I knew that my destiny was to influence a generation to create their own opportunities, to shift the paradigm in the African American community, and to empower African American women to take their financial destiny into their own hands, I had no choice but to rise above. If that is what I'm destined for, then overcoming these obstacles are small feats in comparison.

That is why you must have vision. That is why you have to write it down, make it plain, and keep it in your eye gate and ear gate constantly.

> **The only limitations that you really have are your belief systems, the amount of effort you put into accomplishing your vision-oriented goals, and the financial standards that you set for yourself and hold yourself accountable to.**

Never forget that what you are destined and determined to accomplish is much bigger than some measly debt. You just have to raise your head high enough to see that and educate yourself enough to change it.

Now, I am not saying that having a vision magically makes everything easy. When I was following my own vision, there were still days when I felt like the whole world was plotting against me, days when I felt like I was the only thing on the enemy's agenda. But I also realized that this is because the enemy doesn't want people to be financially free. He doesn't want people to be financially independent. The enemy comes at you hardest when you have a calling in your life, especially when that calling involves changing the lives of many for the better. However, that is what I am doing and what I am urging you to do. So, fair warning: Don't be afraid to almost drown when your calling is to make waves.

Financial freedom is really about having control over your money and your financial future. However, the wealthy are proactive about this. They desire to control their wealth, and they realize that this requires specialized education. That is why, no matter how wealthy Robert Kiyosaki becomes, he and his wife constantly attend new mastermind classes, study under new people, and hone their craft. Admitting that you don't know it all keeps you from becoming complacent. The world is always evolving. Therefore, you should be too.

People with a poor man's mindset have a microwave mentality. They are always looking for the next way to get rich quick with minimal effort. News flash: If it were that easy, everyone would be rolling through the McDonald's drive-thru in Maseratis. You cannot be so quick to hand over control to someone else because you can't be bothered with something that seems difficult or time-consuming. How can you expect results different from those of most others when you are doing the same thing that most people are doing?

Last week, we spent $25,000 enrolling our son in a stock market investing education course. This course will equip our son with the tools, knowledge, and experience he needs to multiply the earnings of all companies under Holland & Holland Enterprises, regardless of market conditions. How many of you paused after that first sentence? How many of you don't even remember what the next sentence said because you are still hung up on the $25,000 price tag? That's okay. It's natural, but it's a habit that I will teach you to break. A poor man is concerned with price; a wealthy man is concerned with value.

Many people believe that if you can't flex in it, do donuts in it, or post it to the gram, it isn't worth the price tag. The wealthy realize that, in fact, the exact opposite is true. To the wealthy, knowledge is an invaluable asset, and they know that all the tangibles come as by-products of investing in knowledge and self-development. If a class was titled "How to turn your Toyota into a Bugatti with these three words," your checkbook might be out faster than you thought possible. You have to get rid of that scarcity mindset, the mindset that you have to eat quickly before your food is taken from you, the mindset of immediate gratification. Wealth is a game of chess, not checkers. It is time that we stop acting as pawns, moving one step at a time, and start conducting ourselves like the kings and queens that we are.

Now, back to this idea of control. The $25,000 price tag is enough to scare away those who are not serious about taking control of their financial future. But with the impending market crash looming in the near future that may rival the Great Depression, I realized that it was a small price to pay. Through this course, our son will learn how to not only preserve our wealth during the crash but to multiply it. People fear market crashes because they cannot control what happens to their money. However, education on stock options, futures, and forex give you the opportunity to take back that control by giving you options for making money whether the market is up, down, or even sideways.

What is $25,000 when there are millions on the line? In adventure movies, is it ever easy to make it to the treasure? Is the treasure ever unguarded? No. There are many monsters and intimidating obstacles littered along the path intent on making you give up, on disposing of or weeding out those who are not serious in their resolve or who don't see the true value of what they are fighting for. A price tag is the first monster you face along the journey to uncover knowledge that will bring you wealth beyond your wildest dreams. Do not let it stand in the way.

Some of us have the money but simply choose to be irresponsible with it. For those of us with more a tangible issue (as in lack of tangible funds), the answer seems to be not as clear. However, it is still the same. You find a way, or you make a way. Use your creativity, use your free time, use your ingenuity, and make it happen. When Rob and I were starting out, we did everything from selling fish dinners in my mother's front yard to selling frozen desserts to pay our children's private school tuition. I didn't bust my butt and graduate from college with a degree in accounting to do that crap, but I did it because I had a vision in mind—one of a better future for my kids in which they started off with connections inside of the white picket fence. It wasn't just an education; it was an investment. Rob and I saw the value, not the price tag.

Whatever money you have, it will eventually rise or fall back to the level of your wealth belief system or your money blueprint.

CHAPTER 4

Defining Wealth and Epigenetics

One of the main goals I hope for you to achieve by the time you finish this book is for you to learn reformed definitions of financial terms that are abstract, yet seem so simple. For example, if I asked you to define wealth, what would you say? Is wealth based on net worth? Is it based on the inheritance you leave your kids? Is it based on the knowledge you have been able to amass? I could ask a hundred different people and get a hundred different answers. The truth is, it varies for everyone. But the way you measure wealth yourself, and your specific interpretation of what true wealth is, will give you a key insight into what your ultimate goals are in life and business, and what you are truly striving toward.

For me, *true wealth is measured in time and not money. It is how long you can maintain your preferred or ideal standard of living without having to actively work to bring in income.* Without pinching pennies or using coupons, how long could you maintain your "best life"? Some people might be two-weeks wealthy by this measure, others might be two-months wealthy, and others might be 20-years wealthy.

When you look at Robert Kiyosaki's cashflow quadrant (I will be referring to this a lot, so if you do not have it memorized, you should read the book and go to Google Images to get a visual of what I am referring to) – he explains that people fit into four categories: A person that is a W-2 Employee making earned income only; another quadrant houses the people in the quadrant for self employed people; the third quadrant is for people who have established business systems and have created jobs in the market place and the last quadrant is for people who are investors in one of the six asset classes and their income is derived from assets. When we look at the employee versus the self-employed person - even as a self-employed person, if I have not set up a business system to run (whether I'm actively involved in it or not), I can't go off to Bali for a year, or even for a month. Wealth means being able to do what I want, when I want, with who I want, without any change to my standard of living. The true essence of working is trading time for dollars. It may sound simple, but you need to grasp this concept at its core. Wealth is measured in time and not money. True wealth allows you to take that exchange of time for dollars out of the equation. Life is one big equation, with a whole lot of variables. However, we all want the same result: happiness and fulfillment. By the time we take our last breaths, everyone on this Earth wishes nothing more than to feel like their lives were worth something, and despite the highs and lows, that it was all worth the ride. True wealth is being able to remove the time-for-money exchange portion of this equation, which gives you the freedom to focus on other parts of the equation that will get you to the desired outcome: happiness and fulfillment.

When you have free time to pursue your heart's desires without having to worry about compromising your standard of living, that is when you will truly begin to explore and fulfill your heart's desires. I love to travel. One day, I want to be able to take my husband and set sail from island to island until I get burnt to a crisp or find one so nice that I never want to leave, and so I buy it. (That's on my bucket list, by the way. I'm going to buy an island!)

I love to travel, and I love new experiences. I love creating memories with my family and defining meaningful moments in time. That is why I am working to create wealth systems that will operate independently of me being there. For you, this might mean running free financial education courses for athletes preparing to play at the D1 collegiate level. Maybe you are a successful career athlete who retired, invested, and can now live comfortably without ever lifting a finger ever again. But it was a long road for you to get there, one that could have been much easier if you had learned early on what to do and not to do with your money. Now, you can go about changing the lives of thousands of kids because that is what brings you joy and fulfillment.

Let's get this straight. Wealth does not look like a certain house in a certain zip code with a certain car parked out front. I know people who live in some of the wealthiest zip codes in the US but who aren't free to do what they truly desire to do because they work so often. What gets us warm and fuzzy inside differs from person to person. But one thing that remains the same across each one of our life equations is the desire for freedom. For me, living a life of freedom allows me to define my life by what matters to me. You can only truly achieve that freedom, to the utmost potential, when you are able to remove the time-for-money exchange from the equation. That is why wealth is measured in time, not money: because time is the freedom we are all so desperately working for, the time to do what we want to define our lives and our legacies. Wealthy people use money to buy back their time.

I was in the UK recently, and a little girl came up to me and asked, "Are you minty?" I had no idea what that meant, and flashed a confused look before she repeated, "Are you minty?" Her mother, who was holding her hand, then spoke up to explain. "She means, 'Are you wealthy?'" I responded to the little girl asking what would make her ask me that. She pointed to my Louis Vuitton purse and Gucci belt. I proceeded to tell the little girl that those things are not what wealth is. These objects being in my possession do not mean I was wealthy. It simply means that I had the ability to either charge, pay for, or steal them. Now, excluding any thieves thriving off five-finger discounts, there are two options, neither of which requires wealth.

So, I sat them down for lunch, and it became a teachable moment. I began by telling them that there are three different types of income: earned, passive, and portfolio.

Earned income is what you make by actively working on the job. Whether you are self-employed or employed by someone else, earned income is that which you receive when you are trading your time for money, like we discussed previously. This is what we are taught to strive for and maximize. You go to school, get a good job, work your way through the ranks if you can, save, live below your means, and hopefully find yourself able to retire. Passive income is just as its name implies. It is income that you do not have to actively work for. This is the income that you receive when you own a business that sells products or provides services that do not require your effort to be carried out. Portfolio income is the money you make in the form of dividends from stock market investments.

The current school system focuses only on teaching kids how to make earned income. It teaches children how to be employees. It teaches kids how to pass tests, not real-life experiences. They do not focus on passive income or portfolio income—the two forms of income that are the most important in establishing sustainable wealth systems that allow us to stop trading time for money and achieve the freedom we strive for. To make matters worse, earned income is the highest taxed of the three. In other words, the type of income that you have to work the hardest to make is also the form you get to keep the least of. If something smells fishy, it's because they've been playing Finding Nemo with your hopes and dreams, and you are nowhere near 42 Wallaby Way, Sydney, Australia.

To put it in layman's terms, we are being bamboozled. Society feeds us a script from birth, and only those brave enough to deviate from this script achieve true freedom, wealth, and fulfillment. The majority of people go through life pursuing only earned income, even though it is the costliest and the least fruitful. Earned income practices allow you to acquire money. Passive and portfolio income practices allow you to maintain, multiply, and maximize your money. Passive and portfolio income take every dollar you make through earned income and turn it into three dollars or five, or a hundred.

Not only that, but the government rewards those who make passive and portfolio income. They subsidize business owners, real-estate owners, those who create employment and housing opportunities. People hate on those in the upper class, like Bill Gates or Warren Buffet, who make fortunes, yet seemingly pay only pennies in taxes. I'm not mad at them; I want to know how they do it! Everyone has an opinion on how the world should be. It is fine to wish the world was a better place than it is. In fact, I pray for that every single day. However, in the meantime, the world is how it is. Donald Trump is president. Is that how I think it should be? Do not even get me started. Does that mean that during the four—God forbid eight—years he is in office I'll just sit on my hands crying about it? NO! I will work to figure out how to leverage these circumstances for my gain!

The word says that the wealth of the wicked is set up for the righteous, yet we seem too righteous to take it. Figure out what the wealthy are doing, copy that, then use the wealth you make from those practices to turn your wish for change into a reality, but do it with integrity. The Bible says, "NO ONE LISTENS TO A POOR MAN, THOUGH HE MAY HAVE THE MOST WISDOM OF ALL." So, this is why it's important that you define wealth on your terms and use it to create change in our communities and in our world.

Exhales

Sorry for the rant; back to passive and portfolio income. These are the kinds of income our kids should be learning about. If they aren't learning it in school, which they aren't, it is your job as parents to be teaching them at home. That is why it is important for you to educate yourself through books like this one, mastermind courses, conferences, and speaking events. Learn how to create wealth systems, if not for yourself then for your children. It is next to impossible to become truly wealthy off of earned income alone (keep in mind our definition of wealthy). I once heard someone say that looking to create wealth from working a job is like looking for the ocean in the middle of Nebraska—it just doesn't exist.

Now to some, knowing the true definition of wealth doesn't seem important. You may say, "Who cares if I am creating wealth systems, as long as I have money? Why can't I just make a whole bunch of money at one time, like by signing a record deal or an athletic contract, or by hitting the lottery so I can live off it without worrying about investing and assets?" This brings about the larger overall question of what type of risk is posed to this nation and its people if they do not understand the true definition of wealth. Easy. The socio-economic divide will continue to grow. Unbroken cycles will repeat themselves. Unbroken cycles, generational curses, whatever name you know them by, cycles of poverty and the mindset associated with them will not only continue but will magnify, given the changing external influences. My grandpa used to tell me, "What you do in moderation, your kids will grow up to do in excess." So, poverty, on a grand scale, is generational.

Undisturbed, a poor family with a poor mindset will continue to be poor generation after generation. However, due to globalization, artificial intelligence, automation, outsourcing and specialization, international competition, increasing education costs, and a number of other factors, the wealth gap is widening. There are more college graduates coming from outside of the US and EU than ever before. We see machines replacing more and more humans in increasingly complex jobs every day. These factors are causing the poor to become poorer and the rich to become richer. If the people of this nation do not realize what true wealth is and do not begin to strive to achieve true wealth instead of the "faux wealth" or virtual wealth we see in movies and music videos, the middle class will eventually disappear even further, and the lower class will sink much further than ever before. We cannot allow our kids to start from ground zero like we did.

We have the power to break those habits and pass on a different financial blueprint to our kids. Actively teach them what true wealth is so that the world doesn't teach them for you. If you want them to achieve something different, you have to show them something different, because my grandfather's quote still holds true in both a positive and negative direction. What you do in moderation, your children will do in excess. The precedent my husband and I have set for our kids and my thoughts about the future that they will pave makes my hair stand on end.

Epigenetics: Your Real Money Blueprint

I strongly believe that poverty is a generational curse, but it was only recently that I discovered the tangible science behind the phenomenon. While the primary reason poverty is generational is that a poverty mindset is passed down from parent to child based on the parent's financial actions, beliefs, and teachings, there is also a genetic component.

What I am referring to is called "epigenetic inheritance," a concept that blew my mind when I first became aware of it. Epigenetics is the study of how one's DNA is packaged and how that affects an organism, rather than actual changes in the DNA itself. I won't get deep into it (frankly, I was lost when my son Adam started to try to get real Bill Nye on me about it). But DNA can be packaged in different ways, and therefore can be expressed in different ways without the DNA itself actually being changed. The way DNA is packaged and expressed can actually change based on the environment. For example, individuals that go through very traumatic experiences may be influenced by those experiences so deeply that their

DNA markers change and are packaged and expressed in a different way. These markers are then passed down to the next generations.

In the case of African Americans, this all has its roots in slavery. There are studies centered on the lasting effects that slavery and the slave trade had on slaves and their descendants. The re-packaging of their DNA was due to the traumatic experience of being shipped across the world, going days without food, being chained to each other and covered in human waste. It was due to watching their parents killed in front of them for the sake of remaining submissive to their masters. I do not bring this up to affect feelings of racial tension; I do it to demonstrate how these experiences were enough to change our ancestors at the most microscopic of levels.

When you think about how traumatic slavery was, you realize that slaves were merely trying to survive. Yet today, we wonder why we still have a survival mindset when it comes to our money. We can't see beyond surviving and subsisting. I meet with some people who cannot comprehend the idea of being out of debt, having wealth, and passing down generational wealth because they cannot see past how they are going to survive tomorrow. Research shows that markers can go back more than five generations, so if something happened in your great or your great-great-grandmother's life, those markers could still be influencing you to this day. African slaves' heads were beaten down so low that, even today, some of their descendants cannot lift them high enough to see the opportunities now available to them.

Such people cannot see their opportunities because their DNA is packaged in a way that predisposes them to have a poverty mindset. Notice the particular wording, however: Many of us are PREDISPOSED to certain things. That does not mean we are GUARANTEED to experience certain outcomes, only that we have a higher chance of experiencing them. It is like high blood pressure. High blood pressure has a genetic link, but that does not mean you are guaranteed to have it just because your parents did. You may just be more susceptible to it than others, meaning you have to work harder than others might to stay healthy. Some people may be able to eat what they want and never have to worry about their blood pressure, while you may have to actively exercise and watch what you eat in order to keep your numbers within a healthy range. The same goes for epigenetics and a poverty mindset.

This past summer, I was speaking at a conference in Virginia Beach. I did not realize at the time that there was a scientist in the audience. I was telling a story about a conversation I had with my oldest, Adam, and my youngest, Zoe. I told the audience how sometimes I felt that my children were extremely ungrateful. Then, my son said something very powerful. He said, "Mom, you tell us how you worked several jobs in school and how you did this and that. I can't relate to the things that you're talking about because that's not my story." This is true. Their story is completely different from their father's and mine. Adam doesn't have the same story, and I didn't realize it until I considered the depth of his statement.

That scientist in the audience explained to me that it is possible to rewrite or reconstruct the way your DNA is packaged. Just as intense psychological trauma can cause intergenerational epigenetic effects, so can that packaging be altered again. I grew up in survival mode. I was too worried about my next meal while I was in college to have anxiety. I worked three jobs, was married, and was pregnant with my first child. Where do you see time for anxiety in that schedule?

But my children are different. I do not believe that they were passed on these gene markers of struggle, of instinctive survival, of a scarcity mindset. Now, I'm no scientist, and the field of epigenetics is relatively young, so I don't need all the doctors to come after me if I misspeak here or there, but as long as you get the gist, you'll see that the basis of what I am discussing is true. What you experience throughout your lifetime based on your diet, environment, stress, habits, etc. affect how your DNA is packaged. If you have twins and one is an alcoholic who finishes a bottle of vodka a day, that twin's body will look and operate very differently than that of their twin by the end of their lives. Their DNA and the proteins they produce to be accustomed to that diet are also different. Then, they may pass on these same markers on to their kids, who might be more or less inclined to pick up the bottle.

But back to my children: They have never had to experience struggle. Yes, sometimes they act spoiled, but I never wanted my kids to experience struggle. When Rob and I were locked in an intense legal battle with our home builder who stole a fortune from us, the kids didn't know it. Whenever things were so tight and all we could do was lay in bed and look into each other's eyes to keep ourselves from crying, they didn't know it. Our story of struggle is not their story. All of the problems they grew up with were internal and psychological. When you don't have to worry about where your next meal is coming from, it frees up your mind to be concerned with more abstract ideas like weighing yourself against your peers, comparing someone else's highlights to your behind-the-scenes life like social media compels us to do. My problems growing up were not their problems, and who knows, I could have passed down re-packaged genes to them so that they do not have the same scarcity attitude that I had.

My children grew up understanding that they can create their own opportunities and establish their own wealth systems. They had a blueprint for doing it, and they saw their parents live it out every day. They saw us find a way or make one, and as a result, even in the market crash of 2008, they never wanted for anything. Money was always around for them.

So, as a side note to parents reading this, before you tear down your child by calling them weak or soft for experiencing things like anxiety or depression, remember that they have a different story than you. You have worked hard so that they may start on a higher level than you did. But with each higher level comes a different set of obstacles that are most often completely different than previous ones. Over the two decades or so that you worked on your mindset, you've totally changed your financial DNA, and the environment your kids' DNA has been expressed in is not the same as yours was. My kids have prosperity in their DNA. They have wealth in their DNA. That is something I confess every day and something that I would urge you to speak to your children, god-children, nieces, and nephews about. Your speaking it into existence, coupled with your actions and teachings regarding a wealthy mindset can work to undo and rewrite any intergenerational epigenetic trauma that might be holding them back.

While, as African Americans, we may have genes that predispose us to have a poverty mindset, that does not mean we cannot work hard to move past that. Just as countless people have gone from rags to riches and overcome the poor mindset taught to them by their parents, so can people move beyond what is encoded in them and pursue the opportunities a wealthy mindset can afford you. Do not use your circumstances as an excuse.

I did not bring this information to light so it can be used as another reason at the family reunion to go on about how life isn't fair for the black man or woman. I bring this to your attention first and foremost because knowledge is power. The more that you understand about yourself, the better you can tailor your actions to give yourself the best chance of success. If you know you are hardwired for a more sensitive fight or flight response because your ancestors were slaves and had to live life on edge, you can keep that in mind and make better effort to keep your composure in high-tension situations. Once you know why you feel how you feel, it is easier to acknowledge your feelings and move past them. Just like we learned from Helen Keller, it is never too late to write another ending to your story, and in this case, the stories of those who come after you too.

PART 2

Cultivate (Create) the Life You Want

CHAPTER 5

Environment

When I was pregnant with my daughter, I used to go to this development full of mansions. At the time, we couldn't afford to live there. We weren't even close. But I would take my brown paper bag lunch, and I would sit in those model homes. The people who worked in the model homes even knew my name. I would go into the living room of one of these houses, put my lunch out on the ottoman and eat. Now, I don't know if they will still allow you to do the same today. Things were a lot looser back then. But I did this every single day for months because I needed to get something different in my eye gate. Fast forward three years later, and I was building a house that was bigger than any of the houses in that development. Furthermore, I was doing so on land that I paid CASH for. If I hadn't spent months feeding that into my eye gate, I never would have established a broader vision for myself that eventually manifested as a longing in my heart and materialized into a breakthrough in my life.

One important part of changing your mindset, your vision, and your exposure, is your environment. Wealthy people operate in different environments than poor people. Before you feel like you belong among the wealthy, you must position yourself there to soak up that mindset and that vision. You have to actively work to change your environment for your calling and your blessings to even begin to work in your life. For you to begin learning and exposing yourself to more, you have to put yourself in an environment of more.

My grandpa used to say, "If you got to ride the bus, get on that bus like you own the bus." So, I have always had that mentality. Even if being poor is your current, it does not have to be your forever. Seasons change. But it won't happen naturally. You have to put in the effort to change them. Nature will not flip the switch for you. You have to be relentless in your work ethic and your vision. You have to literally be a force of nature. It all begins with your mentality and what you attract. I attract wealth, not just riches, or a couple "bands." I am talking generational wealth. I had to get comfortable with that.

Normally, when I get on a stage, one of the first things I ask is: How many of you guys want a little bit more money, or a lot more money in your lives? Everyone laughs and looks around, and people tend to raise their hand for a little more money, but only a few admit to desiring a lot more. Most people desire to be wealthy but are not really comfortable with the prospect. That can be for a variety of reasons, maybe you don't know what you would do with the money, maybe you like to think that you've already "got it like that" and you don't need much more. Whatever the reason, it is stalling you from attracting the wealth that is out there waiting to be seized.

You have to walk wealthy, talk wealthy, believe wealthy, and you will start to see your environment begin to match your mentality. This is because you will start to believe deep within yourself that you are wealthy and that wealth is what you're destined for. Once that becomes ingrained in you, it will drive you toward behaviors that will allow you to materialize on the outside what you already have solidified on the inside. You will desire to create wealthy habits that validate those feelings and your yearning to be wealthy. You have to claim it. Claim your vision, and you will feel driven to have that vision materialized. But, again, nothing comes without a challenge.

Environmental Inventory

The people you hang around also constitute your environment. Your friends, your family, your tribe. It has been claimed that you are the average of the five people you spend the most time with. So, if you surround yourself with average people, how can you expect to be anything more than average?

I learned very early on when Rob and I started building how important our environment was. I didn't notice as much at the time how I was actively working to change my environment. But I did know that we all only have 24 hours in a day, and I was actively looking to maximize what I accomplished during my 24.

So, I did a time audit, and I did a friend audit. How was I spending my time each day and each week? Who was I spending that time with? What were we doing? Just as you are the average of the five people you spend the most time around, the same goes for your finances. Your finances, as well as your money mindset, are the average of the five people you spend the most time around.

After evaluating how Rob and I spent our time, one of the first things that stood out to me was that we were going out to dinner every Sunday with friends from church. Now, I love all of my friends very much, and my church family is like an actual family to me. This is no slight against them, but it seemed that everyone we were hanging out with was complacent with where they were in life. We all seemed comfortable living life at the same level we had always lived at.

Once I resolved to truly walk in my calling, pursue my vision, and work toward not only financial freedom but true wealth, where I was at that time was no longer enough for me. I realized that I had gotten comfortable and that comfort is the enemy of progress. If I wanted to ascend to new levels, I had to surround myself with people who were at higher levels than me or who aspired to reach those levels with Rob and me. I needed to reposition myself in an environment that supported my expansion. I needed to align myself with a tribe that wanted to grow with me.

Now, that doesn't mean I cut ties with all my friends, and that doesn't mean that's what you should do, either. However, I did start to spend less time with them. Instead of going out to eat after church, Rob and I would stay home reading business books, brainstorming, and coming up with different wealth strategies. I had to figure out how I was going to build what I felt led on the inside to build.

It is easy to remain part of a group. There is security in a group. There is assurance that what you are doing can't be wrong because other people are doing the same and are doing just fine. Well, I didn't want to be fine. I wanted to be wealthy. By this point in the book, you should too. I wanted abundance. I wanted freedom. **Spending less time with people doesn't**

mean that you love them any less; it just means that you love yourself more, and there is nothing wrong with that. You have to learn how to want the best for yourself. You must also learn to have the confidence to pursue it even when your environment and those around you do not. Rob and I invited our friends to come with us when we went to meet with investing coaches. Rob and I invited our friends when we started going to business conferences. But you can't want it for someone more than they want it for themselves.

It is so important to surround yourself with a tribe of people who push you and challenge you. Those are the types of people who will motivate you when you feel like being complacent. They will hold you accountable. They will expect success from you because that is what they expect from themselves. Peer pressure works in both directions. If you hang out with people who have poverty mindsets, scarcity mindsets, and consumer mindsets, how can you expect to be anything other than that?

This is why I am constantly enrolling in new mastermind groups. I don't want to become comfortable in the success I have enjoyed; I have made it this far only because I refuse to become complacent. If you aspire to start your own business, or already have one, surround yourself with other entrepreneurial people. Maybe you don't want to start your own business, and you have a job in a field that you love at a company that you love. Surround yourself with people within that company who push themselves instead of those who take extra-long lunch breaks or who are always trying to escape work by hanging in the break room. You want to spend time around people who are also trying to climb the ladder because only those who want it more than anyone else and work for it will be rewarded with promotions. Surround yourself with the people at your job who enjoy Monday-Thursday as much as they do Friday-Sunday.

Until my vision becomes my reality, in every aspect from finance to the impact I plan to have by leveraging my passion for guiding people toward financial freedom, I still have higher to climb. If the Holland name is not yet a household name, I have higher to climb. Making that change and investing in myself by going to these events not only took time, but it also took money. I had to look for areas in my life that were money leaks, holes I could plug so that I could put those funds toward educating myself and moving closer toward my vision. I remember I wanted to take some real estate classes that seemed unaffordable. But I stopped eating out and I wore my hair in a ponytail for an entire year. Yes, you read that correctly: an ENTIRE YEAR. So, it was not just sacrificing the time I spent with friends, but it was a personal sacrifice too. But you have to be willing to give up being comfortable now so that you can ensure that you, your spouse, your kids, and your kids' kids will be comfortable later.

A parable from the Book of John had a profound effect on me in terms of my revelation about my environment. Outside of Jerusalem, there was a healing pool that people visited from far and wide to cure their ailments. A man had been laying there sick for over 30 years among a multitude of other sick people. The Bible describes him as an invalid who was surrounded by the blind, the impotent, and the paralyzed. Jesus asked the man: "Do you not want to be healed?" The man said that he did. However, every time he got close to dipping into the healing pool, someone would get in front of him and take his spot. Jesus told the man to take up his bed and walk. As the man picked up his bed and began to move, he was healed instantly. As soon as he resolved himself to change his environment, he began to experience a breakthrough. It was the environment of sickness, of infirmity, that was stalling his breakthrough. People will lay in a toxic environment for years, completely unaware that just changing their surroundings can create a huge change in their life. Your financial, mental, and physical health—every aspect of your life— is impacted by those around you. Take notice of that, and if you are surrounded by toxic people, change your environment!

The first type of person mentioned amongst the sick was the blind. When taking an inventory of your five closest friends, ask yourself which of them are "blind." That is, which of them have no vision for their lives? Do they have a vision for their finances? Are they blind to changing global trends? Do they still fail to acknowledge how artificial intelligence, social media, and increased globalization have drastically transformed the job market? Do they see the value of setting goals and aspiring to be more? These are the questions you should be asking yourself while taking this environmental inventory. It is impossible for you to passionately pursue your vision if you are hanging around the blind.

Think about it in a literal sense. Imagine you are on a journey, and you know this journey will be difficult and will involve tons of distractions and opportunities for failure. What do you think your odds of success would be if you also had to lead a handful of blind people? It would be almost impossible. For every one step forward, you'd have to go three steps back just to make sure everyone was still going the right way. You would burn out trying to keep everyone else on track and motivated to even continue such a grueling journey when they don't see the value of what is at the end of it. Separating from that group would exponentially improve your chances of making meaningful progress. However, going on this journey alone is long and painstaking. Yes, there is always a chance that you will make it alone, but more often than not, the odds will be stacked against you. Imagine how much easier your journey would be if you found a group just as determined as you to make it to Point B. You could share your knowledge and tips, leverage each other's connections, keep each other motivated, collectively brainstorm to solve each other's problems, and you would all get where you wanted to be exponentially quicker. That is what it's like when you surround yourself with a tribe that has vision.

The next group of people in the sick man's environment were the impotent. Impotent is defined as unable to take effective action, or to be helpless or powerless. When taking your environmental inventory, ask yourself if there are any impotent people in your circle of influence. Do you hang around "powerless" people with victim mindsets? People with such mindsets believe they have no control over their circumstances, that the world is happening TO them and that they don't believe there is anything they can do to change it. People like this tend to blame the government, the law, the school system, and the salt trucks that never cover the back roads. While all of those bodies may be flawed in one way or another and might be stacked against you, many people have beaten those odds. Racism, sexism, ageism, and classism are obstacles that people have had to face and overcome since the beginning of time. Plenty of people have proven it can be done. You just have to have a vision, the right mindset, and a strong enough focus.

Impotence is also defined as being unable to take effective action. The key word here is *effective*. Do you have people in your inner circle who maybe know that there is better out there but who never take any meaningful steps to achieve it? They are aware of what wealth is and are "awake" to the possibilities, but they are all talk. "Oh, yeah, me and a couple friends are going to go in together on a property in the metro area. We'll fix it up and rent it out. It's something we can pass on to our kids that will keep them close like us and put money in their pockets!" they might say.

One week later "Yeah, man, so something came up, and the property deal fell through, but, hey, if it was meant to work out, it would've worked out, right? That probably wasn't the best investment we could have made, either. Oh, have you heard of this new Bitcoin thing everybody's talking about?"

Yeah, that guy. We all know someone like that—someone who pretends to be all about pursuing a wealthy mindset and establishing wealth systems but who doesn't actually put in the effort through self-education and diligence to follow through on anything. They are full of hot air. They take lots of action, but none of it is "effective action." These people are impotent. They do not make the cut. You are about tangible progress now. Leave these people to do their talking. You will show the world with action.

The last type of person in the environment of the sick man was the paralyzed. People who are paralyzed are unable to move or have extremely limited mobility. Do you know anyone in your inner circle that would qualify? These are the people that are too scared to move. They are stuck in place. One, or perhaps all three, of the types of fear I discussed earlier have them frozen in their finances. They are unable to make any meaningful change in their lives because they are fearful of failure or of how they will be perceived. As a result, they spend their whole life stagnant. Do you know what happens to stagnant bodies of water? They grow mold and bacteria. As life goes on, the regret of what could have been, the taunting remnants of a vision they still have inside of them (but never seriously took the time to pursue) turn rotten. It manifests as regret, sorrow, and depression.

Do not let fear leave you paralyzed as well. MOVE! Move now because once you start moving it is easier to keep moving. An object that is in motion stays in motion unless it is acted on by an outside force. So start moving now, and you will gain momentum as you gain knowledge and experience that, when combined with your vision, will be enough to overcome any outside force that attempts to halt your progress.

You may think to yourself, "Hey, what if I show them what they should be doing? What if I help them? Maybe they won't be as scared!" Some people are so paralyzed, unfortunately, that it doesn't matter what you do to help. You have informed them of investment opportunities. You've invited them to business conferences. You have given them books to read and podcasts to listen to. But they do nothing with those opportunities. Humans fear the unknown. Every species does. It's natural. But I would rather take my chances and try to learn what I don't know in hopes of accomplishing my wildest dreams than stay with the little I do know and operate in poverty for the rest of my life. So, you can pray for these people. Pray and believe that the change you make will stir up feelings on the inside of them to follow suit. But one thing you cannot let them do is halt your destiny and leave you paralyzed as well.

Don't get me wrong—most people are not actively trying to keep you from achieving your destiny. However, there are some who are. Misery loves company, and some of your closest friends would rather sabotage your success than be left alone with nothing but their own thoughts and regret. If you tell someone good news about yourself and all they have are negative things to say, that's a red flag. If you tell your friend you finally saved enough to enroll in an investing course you've wanted to take for years and their first response is something like, "Well, you could probably find all that stuff on the internet anyways," or "For all that money, you'd be better off teaching yourself. You know they're just trying to squeeze every dollar out of you." Red flag! Red flag! Red flag!

You need people who are going to congratulate you when you take steps to better yourself. Better yet, you need friends who will enroll in the class with you so that you can get better together. Just as I mentioned in the chapter about fear, some of these people may be your closest friends. In many cases, they will be your family. You don't have to stop loving them or being friends with them. But if you plan on making your vision a reality, becoming debt free, and wealthy, you cannot hang around them like you used to. I mean no disrespect—it's all love. It's just that self-love is just as important as loving others and is even more important when it affects your kids and the generations that follow you.

So, let's now conclude what we've learned from the story of the sick man at Jerusalem's gates. When taking your environmental inventory and evaluating your closest friends, ask yourself if any of your friends are blind, impotent, or paralyzed when it comes to their financial goals and vision. If they are, then you should not be spending the majority of your time with them. Take the initiative and seek out a new crowd. You may say, "Well, how am I supposed to make new friends who happen to have the same financial goals as me?" You do this by changing your environment. If you start going to business conferences, networking events, and joining Facebook groups, you will begin to meet a whole new group of people who want it just as bad as you do. These are the people who you need to spend your free time with. This journey to wealth and financial freedom is tough if you are on your own. But if you take those first steps toward changing your environment, you will start to see a drastic change and financial healing begin to occur, just as the man outside of the Pool of Bethesda did.

Your environment, in general, is composed of many factors—who you hang out with, where you eat, what you eat, and many more things that might seem trivial. But these things combine to have a strong and compounded effect on your mindset and financial vitality. You may have great ideas. You may want to get out of debt. You may want to start a business. You may want to do all these great things. But there are hidden things that can hinder your progress. So, it is important for you to weed out these seemingly small things that hinder your progress so that you are moving full steam ahead when you commit to establishing a better, wealthier future for yourself and your family. Your environment is like a piece of the wealth puzzle. Making sure you position yourself in the right environment gets you one step closer to putting together the bigger picture of your vision.

The Language of Wealth & Abundance

The Bible says that you shall have whatever you say. Yet, people still underestimate the effect of their speech and language habits. Your words help to shape your environment. That is why people spend so much time making confessions and affirmations, and that is why successful people swear by them. Just as you can speak a life of abundance into being, you can also speak a life of poverty and scarcity into being. Before Rob and I got married, we made a covenant with each other that we would never say we can't afford something. My kids have never, ever heard us say that we couldn't afford something. There were times, years ago, when our bank account was at $0.00, but I would just figure out a different way to say it. I wasn't like, "Look, we ain't got no money, so don't go to the ATM today." I would simply say, "Hey, it's not financially feasible for you to go to the ATM today."

To this day, there are still phrases our children do not hear us say. For us, even if what we were saying wasn't positive, we phrased it in a way that would not contribute to an environment of poverty and would not limit our abundance. If the kids wanted something that we couldn't afford, we didn't say, "We can't afford that." We said, "I'm not saying 'no,' but I am saying not RIGHT NOW." We said this because, even though we did not have the money for it then, we knew we would have the money for it in the future. No matter how outrageous the request, from ponies to spaceships, it was always, "I'm not saying no, but I am saying not right now."

We did not want to limit the blessings and prosperity we were pursuing. We spoke our wealth into existence long before it ever started to materialize. We did this by not just making positive confessions but also by limiting negative confessions. That is one step people tend to leave out. If you wake up every day and make your confessions, professing wealth and prosperity over your life and speaking your goals into being, that is a great habit to have. However, if you go about the rest of your day speaking negatively, all that negative speech drowns the seeds of success you planted that morning.

This is not only for the benefit of yourself but also for the benefit of your kids and those around you. Our kids have grown up in these speech habits, so now wealthy speech is natural for them. They do not have to think about avoiding negative financial language because they grew up understanding its impact, in both the positive and negative sense. So, work hard and intentionally at establishing wealthy language habits. Avoid negative financial language, and use positive financial language to help create the environment you aspire to operate in.

CHAPTER 6

Budgets Suck

There are a couple reasons why I believe budgets suck. We have already touched on the first, which is that budgets are confining. God never intended us to live life inside a box. If we do not put restrictions on Him and all of the things we believe He can do, and if we are made in His image, then why do we believe that we should place restrictions on the way we live and operate?

All spiritual beliefs aside, let's get down to the facts. If what you are making currently isn't enough, a budget isn't magically going to make it more than enough. If you do not have a lot of food, eating less and stretching what little food you have will only have you suffering longer. At the end of the day, if you don't have enough food, you are going to run out of food, period.

Remember the story of the three servants from the chapter on mindset? Another lesson from that story is that our God is a God of multiplication. He turned a five-piece fish dinner into a family reunion feast. He turned water into wine. In essence, he multiplied the turn up! I crack myself up, but all jokes aside, when He created Adam and Eve, He told them to go forth and multiply. He gave humanity a mission that extends far beyond just existing. You cannot multiply on a budget. Budgets are all about addition and subtraction. They are one-dimensional and linear. Multiplication brings the idea of compounding to the mix. You no longer increase value bit by bit, but you do so in chunks, in leaps and bounds. The idea of compounding is very important to establishing true wealth as well as a wealth mindset, particularly when we talk about it within the context of education. I get into that in a later chapter, but for now, back to the servants.

Just like God, the master in this story was all about multiplying. His servants knew, just as we do, that their master was an investor who wanted to multiply what he had. The first two servants had a completely different mindset than the third servant. They had the same mindset as the master. They had the mindset of a multiplier. The minds of the wealthy are constantly geared toward multiplying, opportunity, and confidence. The mindset of a poor man, of a consumer, is always geared toward fear, preservation, and scarcity.

People who rely on budgets to try and reach financial freedom have the mindset of the third servant, who was focused on preservation. He had never had anything before, so once he got something, he was so scared to lose it that he failed to leverage it to its full potential. With every dollar comes opportunity. You win the lottery, a family member leaves you an inheritance, you receive a bonus on your job—these are all opportunities that can either be leveraged or squandered based on your mindset. A poverty mindset would cause you to revert to the role of the consumer and buy a liability—a new car, a vacation—you know, "treat yourself." The scarcity mindset innate to poverty would cause you to be too conservative. You would treat this money like the last chunk of money you would ever get. You would budget it and let it slowly bleed out with the rest of your chances of achieving true financial freedom.

Someone with a wealthy mindset would've taken that money and invested it in assets, whether that involves real estate, the stock market, a business venture, or investing it in themselves via specialized education. That is the true way to "treat yourself" because you are treating not just yourself, but your spouse, your kids, and the generations after you that will continue to reap the rewards of the assets and wealth systems you acquired with the money or "talents" you were given. So, remember: We were created to multiply, not to budget.

Being a "money manager" or a budget enthusiast is as akin to being the man who buried his talents. No, he did not lose them. He kept them safe. He managed them. But he did not multiply them. Many of us wake up and go to work five days a week. The lucky ones actually get to use their gifts at work. But we see that as a perk rather than as the standard since so many of us don't get to use our talents. So, the ones who do are perfectly fine staying in a comfortable capacity that they don't necessarily hate. Oprah could have been fine remaining simply a television host. It would be a great use of her talents, and no one would have blamed her for it. But she multiplied her talents and turned herself into a global force in the world of television, philanthropy, lifestyle, and wellness. She did not manage her gift; she multiplied her gift.

God gives us all a gift, but He does not award this gift simply for our own sake. Just like he did for Oprah, Tony Robbins, and Bill Gates, He gives us these gifts so that we may use them not only to multiply the value our talents bring to our own lives but also to multiply the value we provide to others. As I discussed earlier, those in our society who are the most successful are those who use their gifts to provide the most value to as many people as possible. Many of us go through our lives simply managing our gifts, whether your gift is moving people through the music you create, making their lives easier with an invention you create, or helping people conquer psychological woes that are stalling them from having breakthroughs. God is expecting you to plant the seed that He gives you and to then water and nurture it until it grows large enough to provide shelter and food for you and those around you.

When Jesus fed the masses with a five-piece fish dinner, he didn't tear it up into pieces so tiny that all you tasted was a fish's broken dreams. He used his faith, acted, and multiplied what he had in his hands. Even non-Christian people use faith. They have a deep resolve and know that because of their skills, drive, and specialized education, they can expand their means instead of contracting them to try and "make it work."

In his book *Unfair Advantage*, Robert Kiyosaki discusses the power of financial education, as well as some of the "unfair" advantages the wealthy have that make them wealthy. I put *unfair* in quotation marks because these advantages are actually completely fair; you just have to take the initiative to become aware of them and then educate yourself on how to leverage them for your benefit. Anyways, I highly recommend this book, but, here, I'd like to tell you a specific story from the book that always stuck with me.

In the middle of the grueling financial crisis of 2008, Mr. Kiyosaki wanted a new Ferrari. When he told his wife, Kim, what do you think her response was? Let me rephrase that question: What would your response have been? Okay, now that you have all that profanity out of your system, what do you think Kim said? "How do you plan to afford this? Oops, we can't! Which car are you going to get rid of in its place? What about all the other cars you already have? Do they take husbands for trade-in value at dealerships? Because I have my eyes on a reasonably priced Toyota that's looking a whole lot more useful to me than you right now!"

All of these reactions would be natural, but these were not Kim's reactions. She simply replied: "What are you going to invest in?" You see, the wealthy don't pay for liabilities like we do. The wealthy pay for liabilities in assets. **Their assets buy their liabilities.** This all goes back to mindset. Everything always does. If you have a scarcity mindset, a poverty mindset, a consumer mindset, you are looking to conserve what you have. Wealthy people instead look to multiply what they have. They choose to expand their means. This is a topic I go on about extensively in the program this book is named after: my Born to Multiply Program.

Back to Robert (Kiyosaki, that is. We know what Robert I'm always coming back to—love you, babe ;)). He then proceeded to tell Kim that he had already found a new oil well project and had invested in it. When all the preparations were complete and the oil well produced, the income from the well's production paid for the Ferrari. Experts estimated that the well would produce oil for around 20 years. That Ferrari would be paid for long before that oil would run dry. He ends the story by pointing out that everyone wins. Kim is happy because she has a new asset, and Robert Kiyosaki is happy because he has his new Ferrari.

This is a principle that my Robert and I adopted for ourselves and continue to live by till this day. We want to go on vacation? Okay, I run a quick flash sale on my programs. We do not cut out internet shopping for a month, although he would probably do a backflip if I did. Like the Kiyosakis, we refuse to live below our means. Instead, we choose to expand them, just like our Heavenly Father does, and just like you are meant to do.

Knowing how to create or acquire assets is key because you do not have to "work" for that money. Once you know what you have to do, you simply follow through with that proven method that you already have in place. Once my programs are completed and refined, they run forever, independent of my presence. I have already put in the weeks of research and the attention to detail; that work is finished. But they are assets that continue to bring me money without me having to go out and slave for these dollars. Building your own unique wealth system like that is something I help my clients do individually in my Velocity Mastermind Class (a group that I hope all of you will have the privilege to have been a part of one day so that I may be as instrumental in your legacy as my mastermind teachers were to me).

This same idea of expanding your means versus budgeting is what drove me to purchase the vending machines that I mentioned earlier in the book. I knew I was getting a bonus at work soon. However, instead of using it to pay off bills, budgeting it, or spending it, we decided to buy some vending machines. After a few months, the money from the vending machines gave us the capital necessary to put a down payment on our first property. In my first real estate flip, I made $47,000, which paid off all my debt. My second real estate flip made $500,000. I would not have been able to do that on a budget. I would've remained in my financial cage. A budget only allows you to operate within the same four walls. If it doesn't fit within that space, if it is not manageable via your current means, it is outside of the realm of possibility. But if you learn how to expand your means, you can tear down those walls and create a room big enough to house all your dreams and wildest desires.

Another major issue I have with budgets is that budgets alone do not change spending patterns. Budgets do not address the mindset or the blueprint of the root of your spending habits, why you spend like you spend, and what actions you can take that will actually increase your prosperity and not merely lengthen your financial suffering. That is all budgets do: They lengthen your financial suffocation. Budgets put you in a box. Once you are inside of a box, you can only grow to be as big as that box is. Your growth is confined to those four walls. What happens when you try to grow but are constrained within a tiny space? You can't. You explode because you are squeezed to death under the pressure of your limiting, self-imposed poverty mindset.

So, when you get out of debt, it is not because you budgeted your way out of debt, it is because you grew. You grew and you did not constrain yourself. One can only go about establishing wealth through an inheritance, business enterprise, or investing. Budgets do not teach you any of these.

Budgets only teach you to decrease your spending, not how to increase your means. You can only begin to increase your means by changing your internal money blueprint.

First, you must change your mindset and adjust your financial blueprint. You can then learn what real wealth is, and you can educate yourself about the habits of the wealthy. Then, you can settle on your ultimate goals in life—those which will allow you to utilize your God-given talents to bring the most value to the greatest number of people. Next, you figure out your "WHY," which, as discussed in an earlier chapter, is the deep, underlying purpose behind your aspiration to do what you aspire to do. Then, you go about the self-education process (which should continue until the day you die). You hone yourself and build on those skills necessary for you to walk along your chosen path. Then, you use those skills in conjunction with your natural talents to establish wealth systems that earn income without your active involvement. At that point, you have the freedom to do whatever your heart desires, plus you have built a legacy, hopefully in an area you are passionate about.

That is how you become wealthy in mind and body. You must begin by focusing on the inputs, the thoughts and habits you carry out in your everyday, before dealing with the outputs, like what you spend or how you manage your budget. Without changing your mindset and blueprint, you will shortly end up back in debt. Even if you manage to work your way out of debt via budgeting, which would be a long and grueling process (and, frankly, an impossible process for some given the amount of debt and interest it is accruing), your poverty mindset would inevitably bring you back down.

Budgets are also structured in a way that assumes life is monotonous and predictable. However, in reality, we know life is everything but monotonous. Hurricanes, tornadoes, floods, wildfires, etc. are events that we hope and pray never happen to us but which directly impact hundreds of thousands of people a year in this country. Budgets get blown out of the water in those circumstances. When you lose everything, it is quite literally impossible for you to budget because you have absolutely nothing TO budget. Outside of black swan events like disease, or natural disasters that can turn our lives upside down, there are many unharmful events that budgets do not account for: birthdays, graduations, baby showers, weddings, and many others. The minute you spend for those types of events, your budget is out of whack. Even budgets with which you set aside money for random expenses typically do not account for the fact that humans are social animals with friends, families, lives, and customs.

If I haven't made my point 100% clear already, I believe that budgets suck. You can't have limiting thoughts or live a limited lifestyle and expect limitless results. Expansion is key. Now, that doesn't mean that I don't believe in spending plans. Some of us have horrible spending habits that need to be changed if there is any hope of us moving beyond where we are right now. I also believe that saving is good, but only when it is in the form of an asset-driven goal. If you are simply saving your money to be saving it, this is a waste of time. With inflation constantly rising, each dollar you save today is worth less tomorrow. If you are saving, you should be saving that money with the intention of buying an asset. For example, my youngest son, Jonathan, is doing my Savings Challenge with aspirations of putting his savings toward purchasing his first property. That is a savings strategy I support. You should be saving money that you plan to invest, whether it is in yourself, an asset, or your own business system, but never just for the sake of saving. If you are looking for a proven and effective savings plan to help you make equitable progress toward an asset or investment in your self-education, you should check out my Savings Challenge at http:// lashawneholland.com/savingschallenge/

Out of all the reasons that I hate budgets, the biggest is that budgets don't teach people how to use what's in their hands to create additional revenue rivers. Discovering how to use what's in your hands is your pathway to wealth. I believe that wealth follows purpose. You find your purpose, that reason you were placed on Earth so that you could change lives. Through this, you will find your wealth "yellow brick road." There are only two ways that you can change your financial situation: Decrease your expenses or increase your income. When my husband and I were getting out of debt, we choose to increase our income. It accelerates your path to financial freedom. The quicker you find your "Bankable Purpose(™)," the quicker you get on the road to true freedom, and the quicker you stop trading time for dollars. Your bankable purpose expands your income, your influence, and your impact on the Earth.

CHAPTER 7

Bankable Purpose

One of my favorite and most successful programs, which this book happens to be named after, is called "Born to Multiply." I enjoy this program so much because it is a 90-day course that is focused on helping my clients discover their bankable purpose. If you are alive on this Earth, you have a purpose. God gave you a gift that He intended you to use to bring massive value to the greatest number of people you can. God commanded us in the Bible to go forth and multiply our finances, multiply our achievements, multiply our happiness, multiply our businesses, and multiply the value our talents allow us to bring people. In other words, we were born to multiply.

Living a truly abundant life all starts with understanding the gifts God gave you when you were born into this world, those gifts that he bestowed upon you to multiply in the ways stated above. I like to call the gifts your bankable purpose. Now, I won't get too deep into it—after all, I have a 90-day program on it, and I could write a whole book just about bankable purpose—but as a blessing to those who took the time to pick up this book, I want to give you some information, insight, and exercises that will help you discover, nurture, and leverage your bankable purpose. Hopefully, these will help put you on track to the wealth and success you have always dreamed of.

One of my favorite exercises that we do in my Born to Multiply Program is what I like to call the "Limitless Life List" Exercise. This exercise was originally developed by the brilliant Dan Sullivan with Strategic Coach and adapted by Dean Graziosi in his amazing book *Millionaire Success*

Habits, which is where I came across it. I would definitely recommend this book, as Dean does a great job giving simple, effective success tips and exercises that help establish a wealthy mindset (which you all know from reading this book is the most important step to establishing true and lasting wealth systems).

But back to the exercise. The Limitless Life List Exercise will assist you in accomplishing two things. First, it will open your eyes to what you should not be doing. Second, it will shed light on opportunities that align with who you are and what you are passionate about and which bring you the biggest returns.

The first step in this exercise is to ask yourself what it is that you love to do. What would get you out of bed in the morning even if they didn't pay you for it? What raises your confidence? What are you most excited to talk to people about? What puts a fire in your heart? Do you like working with animals? Are you passionate about the environment? Are you excited about bringing people together? Do you love advertising? Do you love working with your hands?

Now, while this is just the first step in a multi-step exercise, I want to take some time to talk about discovering what you love. Taking a scan of the landscape of your life, you will notice that certain experiences peak up. It is crucial for you to examine and delve into those peak moments and dissect them in order to extract out the key ingredients of what made that moment a peak moment.

Let's say you enjoyed helping your friend's daughter win a bake sale competition. What about that gave you joy—you have to peel it back a layer deeper. Was it the baking? No, you hate the tedious work involved in the kitchen. Was it the selling? No, you are an average salesman, but being out shaking hands and making sales doesn't really get you out of bed in the morning. Was it the joy of being able to help the younger generation accomplish their goals, teaching them constructive moral and life principles along the way? Well, you do love kids. You have great concern with what younger kids get exposed to at such a young age nowadays. You find joy in helping them succeed in activities that allow them to build organizational skills and business acumen. Yes, you love investing in youth.

Boom, there's one piece of the mosaic that composes your passion. Now, this is not a one-answer journey. You need to locate the multiple things that make you happy and combine them with things you are good at and the natural abilities you have, and you have to marry those elements to discover what your bankable purpose is. But we will get to identifying the things you are good at in the next step. For now, simply list out things you love to do.

To give you a more personal example, my son Adam reached a point in college where he had to decide which avenue he was going to pursue. He could either continue on the pre-med track and become a neurosurgeon or neuro-research scientist, or he could pivot toward his passions of business and entrepreneurship. This was an internal struggle that he had been dealing with for a while, but with his major declaration fast approaching, he finally had to make a decision. So, Adam began thinking and taking inventory of himself.

When he was a child, Adam dreamed of being a paleontologist. Now for those who don't know, because I sure didn't the first time he said it, a paleontologist is a scientist who studies fossils. Since he was born, Adam has loved science. He also grew to be infatuated with dinosaurs. So, for him, being a paleontologist was a dream job. However, upon further investigation, he realized that maybe it wasn't such a perfect job for him. See, Adam avoids physical work and hates getting his hands dirty. During his senior year in high school, his class went on a community service trip where they helped build houses in rural West Virginia. Well, as his classmates dug the foundations of these homes in the pouring rain, Adam snuck off to wait in the warmth and comfort of the bus. That's just who Adam is. So, when he found out that being a paleontologist involved thousands of hours of digging in the hot sun for bones he may never actually find, it was a "no" from him.

Adam also did a fair amount of research at camps and internships over the summers in high school. While he loved science (biology especially), he found that the grueling hours of repetitive test-tubing to be tiresome and unexciting. Research meant waking up and doing the same thing over and over again, and he certainly did not like to turn on autopilot and do repetitive tasks. He needed every day to be a new challenge. So, he concluded that he did not want to do research professionally.

After watching the movie *Limitless*, a Bradley Cooper film about a pill that allows you to unlock 100% of your brain instead of the rumored 20%

we currently have access to, he became obsessed with the brain. This was the reason he enrolled at the University of Maryland as a Neurobiology & Physiology major. He also loved Ben Carson, (the neurosurgeon, not the foolish politician who tarnished the other's legacy). His admiration for Ben Carson, the spark ignited by *Limitless*, and the possibility of revolutionizing brain function excited Adam, and he decided that he wanted to be a neurosurgeon. Then, he realized he might not have the stomach to take an electric saw to someone's skull and start digging around in one of their vital organs.

So, what was Adam to do? He enjoyed some aspect of all of these occupations, but for some reason could not fall in love with any of them specifically. What was the common thread that connected them all? Other than the fact that they were all in the scientific field, what did digging up bones, test-tubing research samples, and brain surgery and research have in common? DISCOVERY. It finally clicked for him. Adam was never a fan of the legwork, but he loved the idea of discovering something new that no one had found before. Whether it was discovering a new species of dinosaur; discovering a sequence of DNA essential to a breakthrough in a certain disease treatment; or studying, operating on, and attempting to unlock the full capacity the human brain had to offer, the common thread through all of this was discovery. That was what he loved. Adam wanted his name to be remembered, and the way he was going to have it remembered was by being a part of major discoveries. But with each of these interests requiring so much time and individualized attention, how would he satiate his appetite for discovery? (And we haven't even touched on his love for business and entrepreneurship yet).

That's when it hit him. He would open his own research lab. He would own football fields of research facilities, in all areas ranging from biotech to aerospace. He would bankroll the research of scientists from all over and be a part of their discoveries! But an endeavor like that takes money—not just riches, but wealth. Where would Adam get this? That's where the business passion came in. Having started his first business as a kid, Adam knew what it took, and he knew that it was possible to do so in a variety of industries as long as he kept up the process of self-education. Adam finally came to the solution that he would pursue entrepreneurship and business. He would start businesses, grow them, sell them, and then rinse and repeat until he eventually amassed a fortune large enough to open his own research facilities.

I just walked you through the thought process of my son devising, revising, and solidifying his ultimate dream—a dream that is in line with his passions for business and entrepreneurship and which will also bring tremendous value to a huge number of people through scientific discovery.

Now, while reading that process consolidated into a few pages, it may seem like it was easy for Adam to come to that conclusion. But it took a lot of soul searching and his tremendous knack for vision and connecting the dots to reach the conclusion he did. It is not easy, especially at first. We get so used to going about our monotonous daily routines that we often forget what actually makes us happy. But I need you to make a list of five or six things that absolutely light you up, the things that you love. For Adam, that was entrepreneurship, science, and discovery. What are those things for you?

The next thing I want you to do is to think about what you're really good at—great at, in fact. If someone were to ask your family, coworkers, or closest friends what you're good at, what would they say? If you are drawing a blank, there is a simple solution: Ask them. Call up one of your close friends and say, "Hey, I know this might be weird, but I'm doing this little exercise and it would really help me out if you could tell me a couple things that you think I'm good at. What are some things that you think come naturally to me?" If they are truly your friends, they will gladly help you out. If they cannot think of anything, thank them for their time and say goodbye for the final time because you do not need that kind of negativity in your life.

Maybe you're good at seeing the bigger picture, planning for years down the road, and seeing the long-term vision. Maybe you're really good at planning and organization, for preparation and making sure all your ducks are in a row. Maybe you're charismatic, trustworthy, good at leading people, and have an intangible quality that gets people to rally around you wherever you go. Whatever it is, everyone is great at something.

I want you to write down what you are great at, even if it seems small or insignificant. More than likely, you don't see it as a talent because it's something you have been good at your whole life, so you think it can't be that special. Well, you're wrong because what is simple for one person is like solving the Da Vinci code to the next.

Okay, now you should have two lists: one which states what you love to do, and one which states what you're really good at. There will likely be multiple things on each. While there could be only one thing on each, that probably just means you aren't thinking hard enough ;). Regardless, for this next step, we're talking money. Not just money—big money. What aspect of your life, if you acted on it, would earn you the biggest check of your life? After all, we are talking about your bankable purpose, meaning your God-given gift that you can leverage to establish wealth and eventually create wealth systems.

Would it be putting the blinders on and really taking your business to the next level? Maybe it would be finally starting your own business and overcoming that fear that has left you paralyzed for so long. It could be that you have a great product but that it's simply not in front of enough people. Maybe your biggest check could come from outsourcing social media marketing to get your product in front of your target audience. Not everyone is destined to be an entrepreneur, and there is no shame in that. We all have different destinies. Maybe the biggest check of your life would come from getting a promotion at your current job, perhaps by making partner at your firm. It could be securing angel investors that believe in your business and are willing to invest in your vision to take it to the next level! Whatever that may be, think through the possibilities, and write them down.

For the fourth step, I would like you to list your wealth goals. Where do you want to be financially? Make it specific to your income. Do you have a retirement goal that you are shooting for? Are you accumulating funds to one day retire your parents if they are still working? Where do you want you and your family to live? How much would a house in that area cost? If you're working at a company, what do you imagine your salary to be after working your way up the corporate ladder? Do you have stock options in the company? How much?

If you are working for yourself, what is your aspired revenue? If you own your own business and have employees, how much do you aspire to pay them? If you aim to sell your company, what is your dream asking price? If you plan to donate a significant portion of your wealth to charity, what does that dream donation look like? Maybe you've lost a loved one to cancer and the reason you aspired for so much lucrative success is so that you can seriously invest in a cure in honor of that person who stood as your "WHY."

Be thoughtful and be realistic. You will get out of this what you put into it, so I need you to really take hold that vision you have for yourself. When you envision your dream profession, in which your God-given talents allow you to help the greatest number of people, what do the financial aspects around that vision look like?

Next, I need you to write down what actions you need to take today to further those goals. What can you do right now to move those aspirations forward, even if it's just by an inch? I'm talking about action steps. These steps can be small and, in fact, should be small at first. Productivity is like a snowball. Once you start doing something, even if it's small, it will cause you to do more things. You will get motivated by this incremental progress, and you will eventually see it start to compound into achievements you never could've imagined at the beginning. You have to generate momentum, and it all begins with that first small step. How do you climb Mount Everest? One step at a time. Starting a business, pivoting to your dream career, changing companies, securing that promotion at work, completely transforming your mindset, establishing generational wealth—all of these things start with the single step you are taking right now by reading this book and doing this exercise.

With that being said, what are the action steps you need to take? Who do you need to send an email to? What activities, either daily or weekly, do you need to cut out of your life? What tribe do you need to attract? Who do you need to cut ties with? You know the answers to these questions. They will pop into your head almost immediately, and when they do, I need you to write them down right away. Don't give yourself time to think or make an argument, such as "Oh, well, I grew up with them," or "But we used to be best friends." If they are not integral to helping you achieve the wealth goals you just laid out, then they are holding you back from the destiny that God has laid out for you. Now, who are you more worried about letting down: them, or the creator of all space and time? Okay, I thought so. Write all these action points down, and make a comprehensive list of them. We are almost done, and you are doing great!

You've constructed a list of tasks that you love to do, things you're good at, moves that will cut you the biggest check, your wealth goals, and action points you will take to move closer toward completing these goals. For the last step, I need you to take a good look at all of the things on your list. Now, whatever is not on this list needs to go on a new list—your "What Not to Do List." I like to call this a "Perpetual Poverty List" because these are the things that will keep you stuck in a never-ending cycle of poverty. This list is even more integral to your success than a to-do list because this list outlines the activities that have been stalling your progress; keeping you paralyzed; and holding you in financial, mental, and, most often, spiritual bondage. If it fails to push you further toward your wealth goals, it goes on this list because if it is pushing you away from wealth, it is pushing you toward poverty. I promise that creating this list and avidly staying away from the things, activities, and people on it will open the time you "haven't had" to take your finances to the next level. Doing this will also bring unprecedented clarity to your long-term vision.

Here are some examples to help you get the ball rolling for your Perpetual Poverty List:

- Going out with friends every weekend
- Eating out multiple times a week
- Spending too much time per day on social media
- Following social media accounts that contribute to the negative aspects of your lifestyle instead of ones that further your goals
- Spending too much time watching TV
- Spending too much time at the gym (unless you're a personal trainer)
- Traveling too much
- Not starting a business because you do not know how to take the first step (or what the first step even is)
- Doing activities, chores, or tasks that take up valuable time you could outsource and use that time to further your wealth goals. (For example, years ago, I decided to hire a cleaning lady. The hours I spent cleaning the house now went toward furthering my wealth aspirations, and I made much more money putting those hours to good use than it cost to pay her.)

- Spending too much time on the internet
- Staying up late at night

Everything you listed is eating up your time. When you see people like Ryan Seacrest, who is on TV, the radio, and in multiple states all in the same day, you think, "Man, this guy must have figured out a way to squeeze more than 24 hours out of a day!" NO. He has simply eliminated all of the little things that make your 24 hours more like an 18- or 16-hour day. All of your negative habits and activities add up. Your web surfing, combined with your social media surfing, combined with your late nights and bad sleeping habits, limit the productivity you can achieve in a single day. Going out with your friends every weekend, traveling, and feeding your poverty mindset by being surrounded by negative people limit your weekly productivity. These things, combined with the activities or chores you could be outsourcing, like mowing the lawn, cleaning the house, washing your car, limit your monthly productivity. So, how many days out of the year in total do you think you have wasted that could have gotten you leaps and bounds closer to your dreams, aspirations, and financial freedom?

This is an important list of things that you cannot indulge in if you expect wealth to manifest in your life. All of these are habits that perpetuate a poverty mindset. Prioritize what is essential, and phase out what needs to be left in your old story. Keep a copy of this not-to-do list with you in your wallet or on your phone, or better yet, memorize it. That way, you can easily realize when you are engaging in behaviors that cheat your future self.

Okay, final, final step (I promise). Beside each item on your Perpetual Poverty List, write one of these five things:

§ Eliminate
§ Automate
§ Outsource
§ Delegate
§ Replace

I believe this step is one Dean Graziosi added to Dan Sullivan's original exercise, and I love it. It really gets into the specifics of how you deal with each of these items on your Perpetual Poverty List. No matter how specific the activity or category, it can be dealt with in one of these five ways. For example, for spending too much time online, you can "replace" it by downloading an app that locks you out of social media apps for 30 minutes, and you then spend that time reading something that will help further your wealth goals. Maybe you "outsource" cutting the grass to the kid down the street, and you use that time for business development.

It is much easier to remedy bad habits when you have a plan to sub them out with something that is actively pushing you toward your goals. Doing this has the double-effect of not only eliminating habits that perpetually keep you in poverty but also creating new, productive habits. It sounds so simple, and once you make it a habit, it will be. But one thing I guarantee is that you will begin to see progress like you never have before. Replacing poverty habits with wealth habits is the key to establishing a wealthy mindset, a wealthy lifestyle, and eventually a wealth system and legacy.

Now, take another look at your previous lists: things you love to do, things you are great at, things that earn you the biggest checks, your wealth goals, and the action steps you can take toward those wealth goals. Most of the world's wealthiest people love what they do, and they are not shy about sharing that fact. They love what they do because they are working in their passion, which is in line with their God-given talents and which allows them to provide the greatest utility to the most people as a result. The fact that they are doing what they love and what they are good at fuels their passion, and that allows them to see past any obstacles they encounter and keep that ultimate vision in mind.

They have all done the research and have pursued self-education, so they now know what earns them the biggest checks. They constantly set new goals, so they always know what direction they're going. Finally, they take action steps every day, no matter how big or small. The more you feed into these activities, the more easily you can realize what should go on your Perpetual Poverty List. Those areas of your life will start to stand out in the wake of all the prosperity, and you can start to eliminate them as you move closer toward your mindset, self-education, and wealth aspirations. I cannot stress how much these lists can change your life if you put in the effort, are thoughtful about your answers, and commit to establishing lasting change.

Keep these lists with you somewhere so that they are always accessible, whether it is a note on your phone or in teeny tiny print on a piece of paper folded in your wallet. Have these lists on you so that when you are confronted with choices, decisions, and opportunities, you can refer to them to see if they are in line with what you love, what you're great at, what earns you the biggest checks, your wealth goals, or your action items. You should tape your wealth goals to the ceiling above your bed so they are the first thing you see in the morning and the last thing you see at night. I am a big believer in keeping your goals in the forefront of your consciousness. That way, you always remember what you're doing it for when life gets hard. Keep your "WHY" and the end result in mind, and all of the obstacles in the middle will become much more manageable.

As I began this chapter saying, discovering your bankable purpose is a process; it took me years to realize what the Lord finally had destined for me in the realm of finance. This exercise not only gives you insight into what opportunities align with your passions, as well as your skills, but also what earns you the biggest check. Furthermore, it doubles down by shedding light on what you should not be doing, which is often even more important than what you should be doing.

Like I said, I have a whole 90-day course on discovering, honing, and leveraging your bankable purpose, but I hope that some of what I have discussed here will help give you some clarity regarding what your bankable purpose is, as well as what is necessary and expendable to you as you walk your path.

Everyone has a gift, and everyone has a destiny. It is time for you to get serious about it, because you were born to multiply.

CHAPTER 8

Rules of the Financial Game

The game of money is just not a game that you or your family can afford to lose. We are living in a totally new economy. What worked for your grandparents, your great-grandparents, and even your parents doesn't work in today's economy. Having coins in your pocket, and lots of them, is one of the ways that you can turn your dreams into the reality that you desire to live. YOU DESERVE FINANCIAL FREEDOM. YOU DESERVE FINANCIAL INDEPENDENCE. YOU DESERVE FINANCIAL SECURITY. YOU ARE WORTHY OF WEALTH. YOU WERE CREATED FOR MORE!

Really, changing your financial blueprint and obtaining a freedom-based lifestyle is about increasing the QUALITY of your life and not just the quantity of things you own. It's about developing the ONE fundamental skill that the vast majority of Americans can never take the time to develop: mastering their money. You can't master a game when you don't know the rules of the game or the best strategies.

See, statistics show that 95% of Americans are NOT financially free. The real secret is that you can't EARN your way to financial freedom. Earned income alone doesn't make you wealthy. So many people are deceived into thinking that if they work harder, or work smarter, or work longer, that they will then achieve their financial dreams and reach their financial dream destination. Your paycheck alone—I don't care how big it is—isn't the answer. Some people may question why I say this. But the reality is that earned income will NEVER compare to the power of compounding. Compounding is the same as growth multiplied by growth.

Compounding is something that wealthy people use to multiply their money and gain more money in the marketplace.

You not only have to hold onto a percentage of your earned income, but more importantly, you need to learn how to MULTIPLY the earnings that you have. Having money gives you OPTIONS. Building on the RIGHT foundation allows you to survive and thrive in ANY economy, no matter what the latest bubble crash is. What's even more amazing is that many Americans that say they have financial uncertainties and fears, yet they have no spending plan or investment strategy.

People lack financial confidence when they don't have a strategy or financial acumen. When you lack confidence about money, this will ultimately unconsciously affect your confidence in various areas of your life. But when you take charge of your financial affairs, and you feel good, and it empowers you to go after your dreams, you will succeed financially when you have knowledge that other people don't have. And the knowledge that most people DON'T have is that you have to shift from being a consumer in today's new economy to becoming a producer, an OWNER—an owner of the two twin pillars of wealth (I'll get into what those pillars are later on).

Many people are investors already and don't even realize it. They are investors in someone else's dream when they spend beyond their ability to pay for something. They are on the wrong side of the balance sheet. This masterclass is about making sure you get and stay on the RIGHT side of the balance sheet.

See, everyone has their own set of financial statements. I have a degree in accounting. I was trained to take care of, and to create, financial statements for corporations, and I was paid a grand salary to do it. But then I realized that not only corporations had financial statements, but people had financial statements too! That's why when you go to take out a loan of some sort, you are asked a million questions. What you don't know is that while you're sitting in front of the financial office personnel and they are asking you questions about how much income you have, whether you're getting any money in child support/alimony, or how much debt do you have, what your bills look like, etc., they are plugging numbers into their system to get a clear picture of what your financial statement. They are assessing your income statement and your balance sheet.

Everyone has an income statement. Everyone has a balance sheet. Your income statement is simply a measurement of the money you have coming in. Your balance sheet is just a measurement of the assets and the liabilities that you have. Your balance sheet tells someone how smart you have been with your cash flow. It tells someone where your financial heart is. It tells someone if you have been savvy enough to acquire assets (something that puts money in your pocket) or liabilities (something that takes money out of your pocket). Then, once they are done, they decide whether you can be trusted to pay back the loan you're asking for. The more trustworthy you are, the less you will pay them in interest. If you have been scandalous with your money, and you've been a hyper-consumer and they see that they can't trust you, then you will pay them more. People with bad credit pay more.

I often say this: that poor people pay more. That's why it's imperative to know how to play the game of money. It's much broader than going to work, getting your paycheck, and then going shopping. You have to know the rules of the game. If you don't know the rules of the game, you can't play the game well. If you can't play the game well, then you don't score. More importantly, you need to know how to READ the scoreboard. If you don't know how to read the scoreboard, then you don't even know who's winning. If you don't have the right strategies, you definitely won't win the game.

That's why in professional sports, if a team goes on a long losing streak, the head coach gets fired. He gets fired because he doesn't have the right strategies to empower the team to win. That's why you need a money coach—so you can learn the right strategies. You have been holding the playbook in YOUR hands, and the results you've been getting are the results of the plays that you have. If they're not working, you need new plays. That's why you need a money coach. What's your score on the scoreboard? It's important that you learn how to read the scoreboard. That's why this module is called "THE GAME, THE SCOREBOARD, AND THE PLAYBOOK."

See, debt is created when you spend more than you earn, so we must first spend less to stop the bleeding. In order to stop the bleeding, you have to BE WILLING and SACRIFICIAL. Most of us didn't get into debt overnight, and most don't get out of debt overnight. This is why sacrifice is needed.

I have a few assignments I would like you to do in this chapter. I call them Scoreboard Assignments because they help you to read the score (and to put a few points up on the scoreboard yourself).

Scoreboard Assignment #1: Track your spending. This is so important. Every time you get on the call, you'll see we're going to track where you're spending your money, and we're going to do something else with it and build it. It's a buildable process. I often say that your spending is really your compass of where you are in life. Tracking your spending is like when you get in a car with a navigation system in it. In order for you to put in the address of where you want to go, the navigation system needs to know where your current location is. Even if you use maps on your phone, it has to know your current location. If my location module is not turned on, my phone will send me a notification that I have to turn it on so that it can show me the correct route to my destination. It's the same with your spending. To identify the best route to smarter spending, you first need to know the ways in which you are spending unwisely.

Part A of Scoreboard Assignment #1 is to track your spending every day for 30 days. Money has building blocks. Tracking your spending is the foundation on which a strong financial house is built. It's the foundation on which your house of wealth will be built.

Now, after you have tracked your spending for 30 days, for Part B I want you to pull that spreadsheet back out because you're going to take a look it, and you're going to look at everything you spent money on and decide if it was a WANT or a NEED. This is what helps you create space so you can have a surplus at the end of the month.

Your needs would be shelter, food, and work. That's what your needs are: shelter, food, and work. A want is anything that doesn't fall into the need category.

Remember, there are no right or wrong answers, here—it's just results. The results that you get grow from the roots that are underground. We're looking at your results now.

Scoreboard Assignment #2: Now that you know your cash OUTFLOW, you need to know your cash INFLOW. Remember, currency flows. Figure out what is coming in, and what is going out. Wealthy people know where their money is flowing and going.

This assignment will show you that you should have a SURPLUS (i.e., something left over, or extra, additional money) at the end of the 30 days. Having a surplus helps you build your financial freedom. A surplus is the remainder of a fund appropriated for a particular purpose. Everyone should have a surplus. Now, I know, just because you should doesn't mean you do.

Now, to help you, I have included a Monthly Spending Plan Worksheet (see the following page).

Under "Income," I want you to write down each person in your home who brings in a paycheck. If your, or someone in your household's, income is variable (I know some of you on the call are real-estate agents or have commissioned-based income), then use an average of what is brought in each month.

Under "Expenses," I want you to insert the appropriate amounts in the rows that apply to you.

When you finish, I want you to subtract your monthly expenses from your monthly income. This will show you that you either have a SURPLUS (+) or a DEFICIT (-).

A deficit means you are in the hole. In accounting terms, you're in the red. You don't have any money left over because your spending exceeds what you are bringing in.

Now, numbers don't lie, but people do. This gives you a clear portrait of your money. What do you see? Again, numbers don't lie; people do. Many people like to pretend they aren't spending too much and ignore their money trail, but in order for you to move forward, you can't be scared of what you see because it's only TEMPORARY. If you can see it, then you can change it. Even if you have a surplus, you can't be comfortable with what you see because, when something better is available, good is not enough. It's possible for you to multiply the surplus you see into something more, and that's the "better" you need to go after.

INSERT Monthly Spending Plan Worksheet

A close friend of mine sent me a text while I was writing this book. She is an executive for a privately-owned company, and she makes a high six-figure income. She was happy with that. But her text was such a blessing to me and confirmation that I am doing the right thing in the marketplace. I'm doing EXACTLY what I was created to do, what I've been called to do. She said in her text, "You bless me to know what's possible. I can tell someone the journey from poverty and welfare to six figures, but you taught me that I have another chapter in my life that I can write, which is to go from poverty into wealth. YOU inspired that in me. I was satisfied with where I was and never thought about seven figures." See, part of my calling is that I am called to help women leaders discover and maximize their financial possibilities.

Many people won't have a surplus, but it's okay. It's not your forever. This simply means a couple of things: either you have more days in the month than you have money OR you are spending more money than you are bringing in. If either of these is the case, then your next step is to cut back and go lean. Go on a financial diet for a season. The target goal is to always create a surplus. You need a surplus to get on the road to financial freedom. Ask yourself: WHAT ARE YOU WILLING TO GIVE UP NOW TO GET AHEAD AND LIVE THE LIFE THAT YOU DESIRE LATER ON?

Look at the Monthly Spending Plan Worksheet. On the far right-hand side, I want you to write a W if the item is a want, or write an N if the item is a need. Write NR if the item needs reducing (like eating out so much).

SURPLUS SECRETS: Skinny Down to Go Up

Excess expenses cause issues in your life and interfere with your financial freedom plan. YOU HAVE TO TIGHTEN UP TO BE ABLE TO GO UP. Remember, you are creating a NEW and IMPROVED money blueprint, and what you build, your children will inherit.

I often get a lot of push back when I get to this with my private clients. I don't care about the push back; I only care about the results. I'm going to ask you the same question that I ask my clients: HOW BIG IS YOUR "WANT TO"?

Some of the most common areas that most people are NOT willing to give up for a season will keep you in financial bondage forever unless you change. Financial prison is no place for your money. You can't multiply when you're bound. Your money can't grow when it's tied up to so many different things. Your money can't grow when it's tied up by debt.

People often send me messages all the time, saying things like "I want to learn how to invest. Can you teach me how to invest?" Well, the answer is "yes," but the truth of the matter is when you have so much debt and you have so much money, and your monthly income is going towards paying off debt, you won't be very profitable because you don't have that much money that you can invest in the marketplace. There are levels to investing. You get the best returns when you put in your best effort into investing in the market, not just by investing $10 here and $25 there. That's why I always tell people who want to invest to first get out of debt because it strengthens their positioning in the market.

Understand that in the game of money, everything is about positioning. It's about having the right position on the field. If you haven't noticed, I'm a football mom. I've spent the past 12 years attending football games. I have two sons. I notice that everything is about positioning. What the quarterback is looking for in the game of football is the receiver who's in the right position to throw the ball to. On the field, there are many people in different positions, but not everybody gets the ball because not everybody is in the right position to score. That's what tightening up in your money does—it puts you in a position to score and gives you an opportunity to get the ball.

Like I said, some of the most common areas that people aren't willing to give up for a season will keep you in financial bondage forever unless you change. Financial prison is no place for your money. I want to ingrain that in your memory. Financial prison is no place for your money. You cannot multiply when you're bound.

Top Areas Where People Can Tighten Up

1. Cell phones – Do you need to purchase the newest iPhone every time they come out with an upgraded version? Earlier this week, I was online, and I saw that they actually have a $1,200 iPhone. That is absolutely ludicrous. For the average person, it makes the same type of calls that a regular phone makes. I have people call me, crying that they're broke as they're holding a $1,000 iPhone in their hand. If it's not making you money, then it's costing you money. My motto is: If it's not making you money then it's not making sense.

2. Mortgage – We all need a roof over our heads. We all need to live

somewhere, but most people don't understand how to strategically buy a home that fits into their financial freedom equation. I remember when Rob and I were first building our home. I bought five acres of land, and I paid for it in cash, straight out. The seller was in distress. I had the cash. He had the property. It was an easy transaction. We went to settlement in a couple of days. When I went to build my house and I talked to the lender (the vice president of First Mariner's Bank), he tried to get us to keep going bigger. He said, "Oh, you can afford to go bigger. You should increase the square footage of your home by a couple thousand square feet. You can afford it." I knew what I could afford, and I knew what was important to me, I knew the types of schools that I wanted to keep my children in, and I didn't want to be house poor. I still wanted to be able to travel. I still wanted to be able to create experiences for my children. I couldn't do any of those things if I was house poor.

I would never let someone else dictate to me what my money is supposed to be doing in the marketplace. Although he was the vice president of the company, he was still a salesperson because his commission was based on how much we spent. If I spent more, he got paid more. Moreover, the bank would get more money in interest if I put more money down on the house. He was going make more money either way. When he went home to his big, old home with his kids to swim in their swimming pool in the evenings, he wouldn't care less if I could make my mortgage payments at the end of the day. He didn't care whether my kids stayed in private school or not. He didn't care whether I took any vacations whatsoever. He did not care. All he cared about, on the other side of that, was being able to make the biggest commission that he could make.

Never allow someone else to police your pockets and tell you what you can and can't afford. With mortgages, I get that we all need a roof over our heads, but it's important that you're not house rich and cash poor. You have to know the difference between getting a loan that's two times your annual income or 3.5 times your annual income.

Most people today don't even consider whether the loan is 3.5 times their salary or not. They just know they like the house and that they're willing to use any financial trickery available to them to get it. That's why so many people were upside-down when the real-estate market crashed: They had gone out there and got these interest-only loans, no-document loans, and all this crazy stuff that didn't put them in a position to win in the game of money. They're losers. They ended up losing their homes. A lot of families fell apart because of it.

I recommend following a simple rule for people who may want to upgrade their home or who don't own a home yet and they want to buy their first home: When you're looking for a home, make sure you're not paying more than 3.5 times your annual salary. Paying about twice your annual salary is ideal. If you don't have that much to put down to make your home affordable, then you need to work a little longer and save more money, or create opportunities to make more money and increase your income. If the cost of your home is more than this, then you have too much home. Freedom is about sacrifice, and sometimes it's better to rent until you're making more money.

I've watched people struggle to make their mortgage payments when they have purchased "too much" house. One lady—a single mom with three kids—absolutely could not afford the home that she was living in. I told her that she should consider selling the home for a season. She became irate with me. She told me I didn't have any faith. To be honest, my thought pattern was something like 'I don't need any faith. I can make my mortgage payments. You can't make yours.' She didn't want to listen when I told her she needed to either scale back or skinny down. She ended up losing her home anyway. It's not fun watching people have their homes foreclosed on.

To restate my rule of thumb, if you have to get a home, make sure the mortgage is less than the 3.5 times your annual income. With all the short sales and bank-owned homes that are out there now, it's possible for you to work within those numbers and still get a beautiful home. When most people fall on hard times and can't make ends meet and get into debt, it's not because they have more than enough money! It's because they don't have the liquid asset of cash available to get through hard times. The biggest hole in most people's wallets is that they have too much house (i.e., too expensive of a mortgage) for their income level.

Now, don't faint if your house mortgage is more than twice your annual income. It's okay. The world and the mortgage industry will tell you to get a home that is 3.5 times your annual salary (or more) and that your home is your biggest asset. That's an absolute lie. The definition of an asset is something that PUTS MONEY IN YOUR POCKET. It's something that brings money in. If I have to BORROW MONEY AGAINST the equity of my home to get money out, then my home is not an asset. That's still borrowed money. It's a liability. It's taking money out of my pocket. How many of you on this call get consistent cashflow from the house you live in and pay a mortgage on every month? I feel comfortable in saying that 100% of you don't.

Your worth is not attached to the home you live in or the way your home looks. Have you seen a picture of Warren Buffet's house recently? This is a man whose net worth is $39 BILLION, and his property taxes are less than $14,000 on a home that he paid a little over $31,000 for years ago and which he still lives in. I have a friend—in fact, she's like a second mother to my middle son—who had a home on the 18th hole at the Congressional Country Club in Bethesda, MD. Both she and her husband are multimillionaires. They decided a few of years ago to skinny down. They sold their home to move into a much smaller home that was far less expensive for them to maintain.

Why is it that wealthy people don't have a problem with skinnying down while people with a poverty mindset want to live in homes that are sucking them dry? I know people who have gigantic homes with empty rooms because they can't afford to furnish them and who use space heaters because they can't afford to put oil in their tanks to heat them. They are what I call house poor. Conventional thinking will keep you in financial bondage. Poverty thinking will keep you poor. I've had people say, "Well, it's too much work to become wealthy." No, it is more work to be poor. You have to work hard to stay poor.

3. Vehicles – I once heard someone say that pride and ego are the most two expensive things to own and that low self-esteem is the most expensive thing to finance. The best car payment is $0, but if that's not your reality, then one-tenth of your annual income is best. For example, if you make $52,000 a year, you can really only afford to pay, at the very most, $5,200 per year (or $200 bi-weekly) for your vehicle. I hope you›re taking notes on this so you can teach your children when they›re going out and looking at cars. If the car payments are more than a one-tenth of your annual income, then that›s too much car. You don›t need it. If you want a better car, increase your income.

Most people scream at me—yes, they actually scream—and fight back when I talk to them about their car payments, but understand it's about FINANCIAL FREEDOM. Most people will go out and buy as much of a car as the lender will allow them to get just so they can LOOK prosperous. I call this "virtual prosperity." It's a depreciating item. It is something that rapidly loses value. I'm not saying that no one should ever buy a luxury car. I absolutely love luxury. If anybody knows me, they know I love luxury. I actually have a luxury car myself, but my assets paid for it. I would rather create a consistent cash flow to pay for my wants than pay for my wants solely with my earned income. When this is the strategy you use, you have no money in the marketplace working for you. That means you are working for your money and that your money isn't working for you.

I remember years ago (I often tell this story), I had a mentor, Pea, who at the time, was a multimillionaire. She had earned her first couple million dollars by the time she was in her early 30s. She did it strictly by investing. Pea told me, "LaShawne, I don't want you to get offended…" (She's Caucasian and I'm not. Obviously, I'm black.) But she said, "African Americans spend way too much money on cars." When she broke the numbers out for me, it made so much sense. This is what she said: "You buy cars way too often." When you think about it, people normally want a new vehicle every couple of years. She said, "If you take the same amount of money…" (say your car costs $45,000 and you get a five-year loan on it) "…If you take the same amount of money that you are spending on that car every month and you instead consistently invested it for five years…"

She then showed me what my growth would be in the marketplace, and she explained how I didn't get any growth from putting my money into a car because it's a depreciating item. My car wouldn't be worth anything if I kept it long enough, but if I took the same amount of money that I spent on that car and put it in the marketplace, I could triple or even quadruple my money in the same five years that it would take me to pay off my car.

I am of the mindset now that I'll drive my car until the engine falls out. Now that I understand the cycles of investing, I want to be able to maximize my money in the market. That was really important for me. When she told me that, it totally shifted how I thought about it because I had been on the wrong track up until then. By the time she had gotten to me, I was already on my fourth luxury vehicle. I'm so thankful to God that she came into my life, stopped me in my tracks, and taught me to do something different with my money. She taught me the wealth pattern of wealthy people.

Like I've said, success leaves clues. I say it all the time. When you look at someone like Warren Buffet, whose net worth is billions of dollars, and you see that he's still living in the same house he bought ages ago, that's a clue that maybe we should do the same.

What's more important: a $50,000 car or your financial freedom? If you play the game right, you can have your assets pay for the luxury car that you want. I'd rather invest in my businesses and let my businesses pay for my whip (as my son would call it) than pay for it with my earned income.

4. Cable or Satellite Television—Cable is the secret financial freedom thief. It steals opportunities. It steals your time and not just your money. It steals the time that you will never get back, time that you could be investing in your wealth plan, time that you could be investing in your personal development.

Do you know that wealthy people don't spend much time watching television? I suggest you keep a television journal and track how much time you spend watching television. Most people don't realize that they watch hours and hours of television at a time. I read online that statistics from the Nielson Report said that Americans watch an average of 34 hours of television a week. 34 HOURS! That 4.8 hours a day. That's more than two months of television a year. In a 65-year span, that's nine years of watching television. That's nine years of your life being wasted. It's possible for you to create financial freedom in less than five years, so your freedom years are being eaten up by television.

Time is just ONE of the costs of cable. If you have children and you let them watch television often, the average child will see 20,000 commercials a year. 20,000 COMMERCIALS A YEAR! You do the math! That means that the average American has seen over 2 million commercials in their lifetime. 2 MILLION SALES PITCHES over a lifetime. Do you think advertisers would spend as much money as they do on TV commercials if they didn't work?

When you watch television, you are blasted with five to 10 sales pitches every 15 minutes. We learn through programming how to spend our money, how to look cool, how to look pretty, and how to look cute. We learn what we should be eating and what we should be drinking. We learn who we should trust with our money. The question is: Would you allow a door-to-door salesman to come to your house every 15 minutes to try to sell you something? No, you wouldn't do that. But as long as the advertisement comes through the television, you're okay with it.

Advertisers spend millions of dollars every year on television ads because they know they work. That's why they call it PROGRAMMING. They know it affects your money blueprint. Many people could get out of debt if they simply just turned off the TV. Stop being programmed by the marketing companies out there. What's worse is that the #1 advertisers are advertising junk food and fast food, drugs, and financial services. And we wonder why Americans are overweight, unhealthy, sick, and BROKE.

Making Your Vision Plan

In the game of money, simplifying your life is the ULTIMATE DEFENSE strategy in creating wealth in the game of money. People laugh and joke about Warren Buffet being cheap. No, he's not cheap; he's just smart. He realizes that if he simplifies his life and keeps it simple, then more of his money can be in the market working for him. It's about simplifying your life NOW so you can have it all later. It's a short-term sacrifice for a long-term gain. People who are broke and in debt are short-term thinkers. Having a short-term gratification mindset is a characteristic of a poverty mindset/blueprint. A lack of discipline is part of a poverty mindset/blueprint. Virtual prosperity is part of a poverty mindset/blueprint. Choosing to stay stuck and not doing anything to change your situation is part of a poverty mindset in a poverty blueprint.

Many people don't move forward because they don't WANT to see what's in your blueprint. When you don't move forward, it's because you have a poverty mindset. If you don't form the habit of long-term thinking, you will never be financially free. If you don't reset your mindset to focus on long-term thinking and adopt the habits of thinking long-term, you will never reach financial independence or a financial freedom-based lifestyle.

Remember, you've got to do whatever it takes to get the results you want. As I've mentioned before, I once wore my hair in a ponytail for an entire year. I didn't go to the nail salon for a whole year. I took my lunch to work. I made sacrifices like these so I could afford real estate bootcamp classes and make the transformation that I wanted to make. At that time, the classes were only, like, $400, but for me, that was a major commitment. I had to do whatever I could do to shift my thinking so I could pay for the classes because I knew that getting more information was going to change my life. And it did.

Transforming from having a poverty blueprint and mindset to having a wealthy mindset can be uncomfortable at times. But you have to dig deep and find a way to win. This book is about implementing the basics so you can win in the game of money. Solid, firm, concrete money mastery habits will be crucial to enabling you to multiply your money and live your dreams. Who wants a flimsy financial foundation when building a beautiful financial house?

You have to have a financial vision for your money. The Bible says, "Where there is no vision, the people perish," meaning they decrease. So, if we flip that scripture, it would say, "Where there is vision, people increase." YOU HAVE TO HAVE A VISION FOR YOUR FINANCES.

So many people right now are talking about vision boards. I don't personally have anything against vision boards. I used to use them myself. Over the years, my vision boards have changed drastically. You know how Oprah says, "What I know for sure..."? Well, here's what I know for sure: In order for you to be ABUNDANCE ATTRACTIVE, you need clarity and not just a bunch of pretty pictures of clothes, luxury cars, designer purses, haute couture stilettos, watches, and diamonds—that's NOT wealth. That's a consumer mindset, not a producer mindset.

I very rarely see vision boards with business strategies on it. There is nothing wrong with that. Again, I LOVE LUXURY. But those pictures don't give me a plan. My vision board consists of Business Goals, Asset Goals, Fun Goals, Education Goals, and Health Goals. TRUE VISION NEEDS ACTION PLANS AS IT'S ACCOMPANYING PARTNER. Faith without work is dead. It produces nothing. I have learned over the years that cutting pictures out of magazines and gluing them onto a poster board usually just hung on my wall and left me just as confused and unmotivated as ever.

While planning your vision is vitally important and essential to your personal development, you have to be able to cast a vision. You can't accomplish anything just by saying what you want to do with your visual picture. You absolutely need a strategy. I ask people all the time: "Even with your beautiful vision boards, do you have a strategy?" That's the difference.

I believe what's missing from people's vision boards is STRATEGY. This is the action word missing from most people's approach to creating their best life. When most people attempt to move their vision from a board to an actionable plan that works for them, they are using faulty strategies. When you don't have the right strategy, you stay stuck. **A vision board without a plan is simply a nice piece of artwork on the wall.**

I HAVE NEVER MADE MONEY OFF OF MY VISION BOARD, BUT I HAVE ALWAYS PROFITED FROM HAVING A PLAN. I think we should call it a "vision plan" instead of a vision board. When you have a strategy or a strategic plan, you can begin to see the manifestation of your vision. Your desired outcome needs direction to go the distance.

Pictures and words on the wall are simply reminders of our next level. They are not the vehicles we use to get to the next level. It's what you do daily that crafts the momentum to see manifestation. So, I would encourage you to work on your VISION PLAN and watch your financial strategy transform and your money grow!

Now, what are the next steps after tracking your expenses and your money? Remember, I told you that money mastery is about building. It's about putting one building block on top of another building block, on top of another building block.

It is a good strategy to pay down your debt with your new-found surplus. I will tell you right now: No, it's not shopping time! I'll tell you the same thing I tell my clients: When you get your tax refund back, it's not shopping time. When you get your bonus check, it's not shopping time. Cutting down your cable bill, cutting down the time that you spend watching television, and thinking about what you're going to do with your mortgage and your car are just a few areas that you can cut in your spending plan. It's a great habit to renegotiate your utility bills annually. I do that anyway. I call up my utility companies every single year and I tell them I want to reduce my costs. I do this every year with my cable, electric, and telephone companies. You can spend an enormous amount of time clipping coupons, but cutting the pig where it's the fattest is what really makes the biggest difference in your finances. Plus, I would never tell you to do something that I am not willing to do. I am not your coupon-clipping chick. That's not who I am. I don't cut coupons. In fact, I've never cut coupons. I don't have that kind of time on my hands. I would much rather spend my time creating cash flow. This is the first and greatest strategy in the game of money.

Once you have made the cuts and trimmed the fat, you can use that surplus to pay off the debt. That's why I don't jump straight into strategies for getting out of debt in any of my programs—because it's a build-able process. You've got to find where the holes are. You've got to be able to plug those holes. Once you plug the holes, you create a surplus. Then, you take the surplus to get out of debt so that you will have more money to reduce your debt because you are now operating from a surplus.

Many people don't realize that building up debt happens systematically. It doesn't happen overnight. You get into debt systematically, and so you have to get out of debt systematically. You have a system of spending more than you make over a certain period of time. It happened when you had a faulty financial blueprint and were operating under what I call "money mindset misery" instead of "money mindset mastery." There's a difference between the two. It happened when your money zones were operating from a poverty mindset.

We all operate from four different money zones. There's the emotional money zone, the mental money zone, the spiritual money zone, and the physical money zone. Your mental, emotional, and spiritual zones actually make up what we see in the physical. If your mental money blueprint is faulty, and your emotional money blueprint is faulty, and your spiritual money blueprint is faulty (meaning you don't believe you're worthy of wealth and you don't believe that it's possible for you to have more in your life), then what you produce in the physical zone is going to be faulty.

To transform and shift your money, you not only have to move your mind; you have to move your body. Remember, success in anything is 80% internal mental psychology, and only 20% is in the mechanics, the actual DOING. So, the process will need to be systematic to some extent for you to get out of debt. It has to be done on purpose, with purpose. Even when you finish reading this book, it doesn't mean you stop learning. Mastery comes from continued implementation and action. I'm going to say this again: Mastery comes from continued implementation and action. I am always, always, always continuing to increase my personal development. Cut the spending, and create a surplus. Take the surplus and apply it towards your debt, beyond your regular payments. If you have debt, then we need to get you to a place where you can pay it off.

So, here we go. There are actually two methods for coming up with a debt elimination plan. If you do not have a get-out-of-debt plan, the process of elimination says you have a STAY-IN-DEBT PLAN. I often talk about how we live in a dual-process zone on the Earth. If something feels hot to you, you are cold. What goes up must come down. East/west. North/south. We live in a world of duality. Therefore, if you don't have an out-of-debt plan, that means you have a stay-in-debt plan. I recently did a survey that went out to over 5,800 people. In the survey, almost 100% said that they wanted to be debt free, but, of those same people, 80% of them didn't have a debt elimination plan. Where there is no plan to prosper, there's a plan to stay in poverty. There's a plan to fail.

The first method is beginning with the smallest debt that you have. Because you have your spreadsheets and previous assignments done, you have your credit report now, and so you know which source of debt is the easiest to tackle first. Here's where creating a surplus matters. You take the smallest debt, pay extra on it until it is paid off. Then you take the regular payment you used to pay on this debt (plus the surplus) and put it towards the next-smallest debt.

For example, let's say you have a debt that is $1,200 and your regular payment is $100. When you tracked your spending, you said to yourself, "Hey, I found the holes. I plugged the holes, and I found an additional $200 a month." Then, take that extra $200 and add it to the $100 payments, and you pay your $1,200 debt in $300 installments until it's paid off. Then, you take that $300 that has been freed up each month from your $1,200 debt being gone, and you add it to the regular payment amount of the next-largest debt. This will accelerate your debt elimination plan. Listen, I don't care about you just paying the minimum. We have to change our mindset when it comes to just paying the minimums. Paying the minimums will keep you in debt forever.

I don't want to hear you say, "I don't have that much extra money." If you visit McDonald's two, three, four times a week, then you have extra money. If you're eating out every day for lunch and breakfast when you're at work, then you have extra money. If you're going to the movies every weekend with your girlfriends or going to happy hour (happy hour is not free hour), then you have extra money. You still have to pay for something. I don't care how discounted the food and drinks are, you still have to pay for something. Again, how big is your "want to"? Eliminating these costs will accelerate your debt elimination plan.

The second method is similar to the one that we just discussed. However, instead of paying off the smallest debt first, you start with the debt that has the highest interest rate. When you pay this off, you move to the debt with the next-highest interest rate, and so on.

Once your debt is paid off, you get to do something way more fun with your surplus than paying off debt. YOU GET TO MULTIPLY YOUR MONEY. This is my sweet spot. I absolutely love teaching this, which is way more fun than dividing. I tell people that all the time. Multiplying is way more fun than dividing. Adding is way more fun than subtracting. Making money is way more fun than not having any. When you divide your money between a bunch of credit card payments and other expenses, you have less money working in the market for you.

The biggest problem in money management is not the lack of money, it's the lack of a SYSTEM. My mentor taught me this. She said, "LaShawne, SYSTEMS SET YOU FREE." You have to develop a system that will track your money so you can keep score. Now, she didn't tell me that part (because we weren't talking about money), but the premise goes for anything. Systems that set you free, even in business. When you know what the score is in a game, you know who's winning.

See, with the progress you are making in the game of money, you won't be able to see it if you're not tracking it. You've learned a powerful defense strategy, a scoreboard strategy, and we are getting ready to tackle on the offense side of the game of money. A great offensive strategy is knowing what percentage of your annual income should go where. This is what I call my "M4 Wealth Strategy," or the "Millionaire's Money Mastery Method.". It's a wealth strategy. While I don't go over every last detail of the system in this book, I will present the system to you in such a way that I think you're still going to be able to pick up on it. There are six different accounts that you're going to set up at your bank. I know that seems like a lot, but there's a method behind it.

1. The Golden Goose Account (10%) – Your Golden Goose Account is your Financial Freedom Account. The money that goes into this account will go towards investing in things like businesses, real estate, and other wealth-building strategies. Once you have paid off your debt, all your surplus will go to this account (over and above the 10% that you're putting in here) to ACCELERATE your journey to a financial-freedom-based lifestyle. It's 10%, and this will accelerate your journey. It's what I call my Velocity Account. It just helps me to get to where I want to be faster. Again, if you don't have a plan for prosperity then, by omission, you have a plan for poverty. This is positioning you to have a plan for prosperity.

2. Planned Savings for Spending Account (10%) – Not having a separate account for this kind of spending is how most people get into debt. Use this account to save up money so you can buy high-ticket items and save for unforeseen expenses that pop up, like a new car, a new flat-screen TV, a new computer, college funds for your children, Christmas funds, or an awesome vacation. It's the account that most people would call a savings account. The statistics show that not many people are saving now. This is called your Planned Savings for Spending Account. If your refrigerator breaks down or your stove breaks down, you don't have to open up an account with Sears, or JC Penney's, or somebody else, and you don't have to charge the expense to your credit card because you have planned for this expense. So, it's your Planned Saving for Spending Account. That's 10%.

3. Investment in Me Education Account (10%) – I think it's imperative that you invest in yourself. Investing in your personal development and transformation is one of the best investments you can ever make. I call this the Investment in Me Education Account. Ten percent of your income will go into this account. This account is used for anything that supports your ongoing education, like books, seminars, bootcamps, teleclasses, master classes, or mastermind programs. Oftentimes, people can't afford to partake in opportunities for personal development when they arise because they didn't plan for such opportunities. If I am going to attend a conference or something, and the opportunity arises for me to do something that I know will put me in a better position to get further down the field so I can score a touchdown in the game of money, I already know what to do

because I put aside a plan for it. I can't restate it enough times: If you don't plan for prosperity, you plan for poverty. I want you to remember that. You have to put money aside for investing in YOU. That's your investment in the Investment in Me Education Account.

4. Fun Money Account (10%) – This is the account you can draw from to have guilt-free fun. Here is where you get to shop for clothes, buy shoes, go to the spa... I have a fetish for expensive perfume. I love expensive perfume. This comes out of my Fun Money Account. You can splurge on perfume or fine dining—whatever makes you feel amazing. Who wants to have a spending plan where you don't account for having any fun? You're not going to stick to that for a long period of time. Being wealthy is about creating experiences. I love to wind sail over the ocean. It's so peaceful up there, hundreds of feet up in the air, just sailing through the air over the ocean. It's one of my most favorite things to do. Well, guess where the money for that comes from. It comes from my Fun Money Account. When we go on vacation, my kids love to do every excursion known to mankind. I don't have to charge anything to a credit card because I plan for these expenses. Again, you have to plan for prosperity, or, by omission, you plan for poverty.

5. Charitable Giving Account (10%) – Here is where you get to tithe or give to any charity of your liking. Wealthy people give. They understand the laws of sowing and reaping and of making a difference in someone else's life.

6. Living Expenses Account (50%) – This money is used towards paying off your bills, your rent, your mortgage, your utilities, your groceries, everything that you need to live your everyday life Most of us are trained to live off of 100% of our income. It may take some time to shift and get used to this goal, but you've got to start somewhere. If it currently takes you 90% of your income to pay for your living expenses, then you need to consider seriously simplifying your life. How can you do that? One of two ways. There are only two ways that you can change your financial situation: increase your income or decrease your expenses.

The best practice is for you to open up six accounts with your bank and make direct deposits into these accounts from your earned income. You can set up automatic transfers, or you can take the after-tax dollars and transfer them into the respective accounts yourself. PLEASE NOTE THAT THE

PERCENTAGES ARE FLEXIBLE. The ones that I suggested are a great target, but always be flexible in your approach. If you're not there yet, start with something, even if it's just your Golden Goose Account. You have to start with something.

Scoreboard Assignment #3: Take your MONTHLY SPENDING PLAN WORKSHEET and mark which expenses fall into which category. There is already a space for you to do this on the worksheet that you can get here: lashawneholland.com/btmspendingplanworksheet. It's located in the far-right side of the worksheet and is marked "ACCT" (abbreviation for "account"). Just put:

- GGA for Golden Goose Account
- PSSA for Planned Savings for Spending Account
- IME for Investing in Me Education Account
- FMA for Fun Money Account
- CGA for Charitable Giving Account
- LEA for Living Expenses Account

Once you've done this (and this is why this is so important), you can see where you are compared to the recommended percentages that I gave you. You'll see that you may be spending 80% from your living expenses account and that after you give another 10% (if tithing is important to you), that 90% of your income is tied up. You have only 10% left over. It becomes very difficult to automate money to go into my golden goose account for my future. Once you do this Scoreboard Assignment #3, you'll see where you are in this. You'll see where you are compared to the recommended percentages.

This entire process of cutting costs, deriving spending plans, eliminating your debt, and managing your money alone has the ability to set you financially free. It positions you to be a great MULTIPLIER. Getting out of debt may take a while, but that's irrelevant. The fact that you now have a plan shows the universe, and it shows God, that you can be trusted to expand your territory and multiply your money into more. We were created to be multipliers, and not just managers. My husband said it when I was reading something and shared it with him—he said,

"Wow, that's amazing!" We were born to be multipliers, but we were programmed to be managers. We're out of position. When all we're doing is constantly managing, we're not multiplying anything. I realize that this process can be a lot and that it can be boring at times, but its better than struggling and being in the same place year after year. Remember, what you don't change, you pass on. What you do in moderation, your kids will grow up to do in excess. That's why, for every generation, the debt gets greater and greater—because they're not being taught these principles.

It's possible for you to blaze a trail where no one else in your family has been before. I know. I have done it, and I'm still doing it. I need my kids to cross the billion-dollar mark. I have to get them as far ahead in the game as I can, so when I finally pass the baton, they can run like the wind. I remember *Toy Story*: "Run like the wind, Bullseye!"

If you can't afford to implement the entire M4 Wealth Strategy, not killing the golden goose is the most important aspect because your Golden Goose Account is what prepares you for your future. Most people don't invest with income in mind. However, if you want to live an abundant life in your future, you have to plan for it TODAY.

It's not a dream. People make wealth out to be this very frail, far-off thing that all they do is sit up and daydream about. Wealth is a choice. It's not a dream. I heard Dennis Kimbro say this at a conference I was attending years ago: "Our todays are what your yesterdays made them; our tomorrows must inevitably be the product of our todays. Those who neglect opportunity and avoid responsibility do so at the risk of any possible financial attainment or advancement." He went on to say, "Throw away your money if you will and waste if you must… your possessions, your homes, your resources… but never, ever discard OPPORTUNITY. No power, no force in the universe can restore to you its value or the possibilities for growth and accomplishment contained within." I thought that was so powerful. It has stayed with me for about six or seven years now since I first heard him say that.

Remember, money (both when you have it and when you lack it) has always been, and will always be, the greatest measurement of your mindset. Money will always meet you where you are. Money is not good, nor is it bad. It's a resource to be used and exchanged in the marketplace;

if we are smart and we play the game of money to win, we get to live the life that we desire. Money tends to flow toward those who can use it the most effectively and productively, to those of us who can seize opportunities, create more opportunities, and ultimately benefit others. That's really what it's about: getting to the point where we can live a life of significance.

PART 3

Grow Your Financial Outlook

CHAPTER 9

Pivot & Opportunity

People who start at the bottom rarely raise their heads high enough to see opportunity - Coach Dav

The secret superpower of a wealthy mindset: RECOGNIZING OPPORTUNITY

I remember reading a true story about the founders of a company you are probably familiar with: Airbnb. Brian Chesky and his co-founders found themselves $20,000 in debt several months after they started the now $25-billion startup. No investors took their idea seriously. Think about it: Before Airbnb, who would have allowed a complete stranger to stay in their house? Did you laugh as hard as I did at that question? HECK, NO. That potential serial killer can sleep outside. Well, all the panels of investors they pitched to felt the same way. After amassing all this debt and being laughed at for months by investors, they easily could've quit. But what did they do? The exact opposite. They started another company.

This predicament they found themselves in was actually happening right before the 2008 election. So, they got the bright idea to create novelty cereal boxes: Obama O's and Cap'n McCain's. They contacted a print shop, had a batch of 1,000 boxes created, and sold each for $30 a pop! With the help of a well-placed national television feature, they sold every single box of that cereal—which were just Cheerios and Captain Crunch, I might add—for $30,000. This not only wiped out their debt but also gave them an extra $10,000 to invest in Airbnb. They were willing to do what others wouldn't. That is why, today, they are accomplishing what others can't.

This story exemplifies the three ideas I would like to highlight in this chapter: Recognizing opportunity, pivoting, and intentional focus.

One of the most important abilities wealthy people possess is the ability to recognize opportunity. They see through all the noise, and when the time comes, their gut tells them that this is an opportunity that they would regret letting pass by. Now, some people are born with great natural ability to recognize opportunity where it is not very apparent. However, there are many times in your life where you, as a normal person, are confronted with a choice. Depending on your mindset, your vision, and your level of education (financial IQ, business development education, etc.), you will either seize this opportunity or let it pass you by (or maybe miss it altogether). Many people pray and believe God for a blessing, but when it arrives, we cannot recognize that the opportunity is the blessing. Our short-sightedness may not allow us to see past an obstacle associated with it to grasp the value of the bigger picture.

I remember when, years ago, Robert and I were in New York attending a meeting one of our mentors/coaches was having. He made a statement that has always stuck with me: "People who start at the bottom rarely raise their heads high enough to see opportunity."

It made me think of an instance when someone I knew wanted to start a business. I wanted to help her, so I contacted a friend of mine who was an expert—not just an expert, but a WORLD-RENOWNED, HIGHLY SOUGHT-AFTER EXPERT—in this industry. She was giving a class, and I called her and asked if my girlfriend could sit in on the class. I knew my girlfriend couldn't afford the cost of the class, so I called in a favor. She said "yes," and I was so excited I called my girlfriend back and told her she could take the class. She told me she had to pray about it. That was over 15 years ago, and she never got started with the business, and her family continues to struggle until this day. That was the LAST phone call I made to call in a favor for her. In fact, it was the last conversation I had with her. The lesson I learned? You can't want something for someone more than they want it for themselves. This was an example of her not raising her head high enough to see opportunity. This is just ONE of the many sad examples I have witnessed of people not being able to see opportunities.

Earlier, I discussed the $25,000 stock market investing class we enrolled my son in. Rob, Adam, and I had attended a two-day crash course in options that cost $1,000. At the end of it, of course, they pitched for us to enroll in the full program—which, for that day only, was discounted to only 25 times the price of the class we were sitting in! We took a break for lunch as the instructor let us mull over his proposition.

Adam was quiet when he sat down to eat, which is very uncharacteristic of him. He normally talks so much while he eats that he is almost always the last one done. Then, he looked Rob and me in the face and said, "I want to do it." I could see the resolve in his eyes. He then explained how he understood that the price tag was hefty, but he weighed it against all the assets Holland & Holland Enterprises stood to lose in a market crash, all of the capital the family had worked so hard to make. He not only recognized the short-term opportunity of us being able to preserve our family's wealth, but he also recognized the long-term goal of being able to pass this knowledge on to his kids. Not only that, but he could also then deliver this message to people at my conferences. He recognized this as an opportunity for him to learn a valuable skill that the African American community, those at my conferences, those reading this book, desperately need. This was going to be Adam's area of expertise and his contribution to our family's aim to shift the paradigm in the black community for generations to come.

I was put in a similar situation years ago, and it was one of the most life-changing experiences I've ever had. In 2011, my sons won the *Black Enterprise Magazine* Teenpreneur of the Year Award. They were in middle school at the time. We all flew down to Atlanta, GA for the Annual Entrepreneur Conference. There was this one particular session that we all attended, and one of the speakers on the stage was Marshawn Evans. I am not sure what she said, but whatever it was, it was enough to captivate my youngest son. The session ended, and my sons had to go do an elevator pitch contest. When they finished the pitch, I saw my son run up the escalator, and I saw him speaking with this woman. Being the eagle mom that I am, I headed up the escalator to see who was talking to my son and what she was saying that had him so mesmerized. She was talking to him about the Award he just won and how he could use it in business for the rest of his life. She invited him to attend her Branding Bootcamp and gave him the information.

When we got home, he begged me to take them. NO. That was my answer. We were paying a fortune in tuition at the time, and they were going to be in school every minute that those school doors were open. It was settled as far as I was concerned. I thought they forgot about it. Then, later in the week, they came downstairs and told me they registered me for the conference. I was SHOCKED, to say the least. The conference registration was $2,000. (You may be wondering where they got the money from, but my kids had made $110,000 with their business, AJ's Hawaiian Iceez, by the time they were 12 and 13 years old, respectively.)

So, I ended up flying back to Atlanta and attending the bootcamp. I sat in the front row. As Marshawn spoke, I cried like a newborn baby. I mean, it was an ugly cry too. I couldn't control it. It was like Marshawn was confirming things in her presentation that I had hidden in my heart that I didn't even know were there. I know now that this is what a "destiny moment" looks like. SHE was the messenger God sent into my life to wake up the dream, but I still had to RECOGNIZE THE OPPORTUNITY. I invested in her $10,000 mastermind, and she has been extremely instrumental in my life and the lives of my entire family since then. If I had never said yes to the opportunity to work with her, I am positive you wouldn't be reading this book right now.

I came back home from Marshawn's Branding Bootcamp, and I told my pastor my revelation and my acceptance of the call on my life. I told him that I was placed in the Earth to teach people how to multiply. I remember after I shared it with him, he looked me in my eyes and said, "I feel the presence of God all over this. Look at my arms. Hair is standing up on my arms. I know this is the hand of God on your life." Now, mind you, I'm the comptroller of all nine of his locations. He says, "I know the hand that God is on your life. I'm a man. I will not stand in your way. You can go wherever you need to go. Just come back home." And he walked out the door.

My family's journey has been full of opportunities that have been presented to test us and moments when we had to pivot. That essential moment is what drove me to where we are today. All the late nights spent developing my programs, working with clients, spending hundreds of thousands on attending mastermind classes and business development conferences, were all rooted in that moment. Now, as powerful as that story is, it could have never happened if Adam had not seized that opportunity to put me in that position, and I wasn't receptive enough in mind and spirit to recognize that I was there for an opportunity and a purpose much bigger than developing my children's shaved ice company. God will put you in positions that catch you off guard. But you have to have the foresight to see and seize opportunities. I was not there attending the Branding Bootcamp for myself. It would have been completely rational for me to bottle those feelings of inspiration up and to tell myself to focus on the task at hand, but then my life never would have changed as remarkably as it did. Even worse, I would not have been able to help change the lives I have as a result of me recognizing the path that was destined for me.

However, the answer to the question you're asking yourself is "no." No, there will not be a big red blinking sign that says "THIS WAY!" Someone will not always be there to take you by the hand and say that something is too good of an opportunity for you to pass up. You will have to feel it—the same conviction Adam felt about the stock class, the same conviction I felt when I first heard Marshawn. When you feel your spirit start to light up, you must have the courage to follow it. There will be sacrifices, long nights, and big price tags, but remember that having a wealthy person's mindset transcends these obstacles. You will recognize the value behind all the noise, and how it is ten times worth whatever time, money, or blood, sweat, and tears you are putting into it.

It's in these moments that I have learned to compare value vs. cost. What is the cost of me NOT changing or of not saying yes to destiny? People are so oblivious to making decisions based on the weight of VALUE that something brings to their lives that doesn't have an expiration date on it. Value is the usefulness or desirability of a good or service, how much you love it, or what it is "worth" to you. Value is not a number, yet people treat it like it is. Value can be useful for as long as you live. You can pass value down to generations. The cost of something comes and goes, but value doesn't expire.

I cringe when people say they didn't go to an event or didn't do something because it cost too much. They don't understand that the VALUE you get from gaining more education or more knowledge can be used way beyond the dates of the conference. When I invest in value, it benefits me for years to come, way past the cost of a book, a class, a mastermind, a conference, or whatever I paid to receive. The value always outweighs the cost because value is not a number; it is the intangible asset you invest in that yields returns over and over and over.

There were also times in life when I was confronted with opportunities that I did not take advantage of. It isn't all roses and inspiration. Just like anyone else, I had my doubts. At the time, I couldn't see the diamond in the rough. I wasn't educated enough to understand the price tag at the time was nothing compared to the value in the future. For example, back in 1995, Rob and I had an opportunity early on in our investing career to invest in property on Capitol Hill in Washington, DC. We were offered to purchase a row house for $40,000. It was in TERRIBLE condition. It needed to be gutted completely. I didn't want it. It was small, and I lacked vision. Fast forward 10 years, the property is worth over a million dollars. I DIDN'T RECOGNIZE THE VALUE OF THE OPPORTUNITY. I can teach you about this because I have made plenty of mistakes about not seeing value. I had to train my inner man to be able to recognize opportunities, and it came through investing in specialized knowledge and personal development.

To chase my vision and overcome all of the obstacles I have faced over the years, one thing I have had to learn to do is pivot. When you come across adversity that is simply too much for you to continue doing things how you do them, you must pivot. Sometimes, there are extenuating circumstances that you simply cannot will your way through. Let me rephrase that: Maybe you can will your way through them, but doing so would take you a lot of time and money, and it might demoralize you enough that you lose that fire for achieving your aspirations. This is when the pivot comes in. Like Kenny Rogers says, "You got to know when to hold them, know when to fold them, know when to walk away, and know when to run."

What I'm actually talking about is your ability to overcome any obstacle. When you make a commitment to change or to transform your money blueprint and to build your version of wealth, life continues to happen even though you have made a commitment to multiply your money and do something that 98% of Americans never choose to do.

Despite what comes up on the journey, I have learned to remain unshakable in my commitment to build wealth without limits while being flexible in my approach. Once you decide to be relentless and to be rich, you will have PLENTY of opportunities to fall off the wagon. But once you decide to be a money multiplier, you cut off any possibility of obstacles setting you back to the point of giving up. Oftentimes, you have to learn to pivot and change your approach.

I used to play basketball in middle school. I was a forward, and I remember one particular practice, my coach made me practice pivoting all evening because I was traveling so much during the game. Pivot means to swivel, revolve, spin, or to rotate. If things aren't going the way you thought, pivot. The founder of the global market disruptor that is Amazon started out selling books, and he built the company using second-hand computers in his garage. He then got caught up in the dot-com crash and had to pivot to stay alive. Jeff Bezos has had to pivot many times throughout Amazon's journey, and he continues to pivot in order to grow.

The concept of pivoting is really about your resilience or your pliability. How pliable are you? How bendable are you? See, we were created to bend, but not to break, when things come up. A lot of times, people think that financial hardships break you, but it's your perception of the matter that causes you to be pliable. You can pivot at any time.

And we are currently living in a society where the art of pivoting is necessary. There is so much uncertainty in the world. People are concerned about their livelihoods and their financial lives. I read a poll that said the #1 thing that keeps people up at night is worrying about their finances. Gone are the days of pensions where, if you worked for 30+ years, you could retire and still get a check for the rest of your life. You have AI now that can virtually replace millions of jobs, and people are ignoring the AI Revolution that is taking place (CNBC and Fortune both reported that China has already replaced 40% of its workforce with robots). You have people graduating from college with enormous amounts of student loan debt, and they can't find jobs that will allow them to pay it back. You have consumer debt rising. There is just so much uncertainty, and where there is uncertainty, there is fear. Just globalization, in general, has changed the game for so many industries. This is why I am such a HUGE advocate of you taking charge and taking control of your own personal economy. You do this by pivoting.

I am not telling you to quit your job. I am telling you to create more revenue in your household in addition to the paycheck you earn from your job. I am telling you not to leave your financial futures in the hands of your employer, the government, the state, your spouse, or your church (the church's benevolence ministry is NOT your retirement plan, so you better not depend on them to help you out for the rest of your life).

Money is only a tool. It will take you wherever you desire to go, but one thing money will not do is replace you as the driver. Today's economic climate requires you to be relentless in building a great financial foundation and then constructing wealth on top of that. YOU HAVE TO TAKE BACK CONTROL OF YOUR MONEY.

I know you may have grown up in a house where no one taught you about money, and we sure didn't learn about money in school. Okay, that's settled. But do you let these excuses stop you from learning about money and building the life you desire? You have to be RELENTLESS in your approach to building money, and that requires you to place one foot on the court and pivot. Pivot from having one revenue stream. Pivot from being a consumer only. Pivot from not having savings or a retirement account. Pivot from not having positive cash flow. Pivot from letting the credit card be your money pimp. Your ability to pivot is the secret power that gives you peace of mind in a world of uncertainty. Your ability to pivot is a STATE OF MIND. No matter what unexpectedly pops up, you will stay on track. You will find a way or make a way. You will have unwavering resilience in the midst of storms that arise. Fear, anxiety, and uncertainty where your money is concerned, past failures, financial confusion, and undeveloped money are all obstacles that you can get around.

Your Perception of Obstacles Makes a Difference

Some people see obstacles as a mystery to solve. Some see obstacles as an opportunity to grow. Others see obstacles as threats. Still, others see obstacles as proof that they cannot succeed. Your view of barriers to achieving your goals affects how you react. Your perception affects every little step you take.

If you see obstacles from a victim's point of view, as a sign that the world is against you, or as an indicator that you have failed, then you are likely to be overwhelmed with negative thoughts and difficult emotions when faced with roadblocks to your vision and dreams.

Perhaps you don't really experience thoughts when faced with an obstacle. Maybe you immediately experience fear or shame (I hear this a lot from clients). But fear tells you to escape the situation; it tells you that you are in danger. Shame urges you to hide. If the situation isn't one of which you need to be afraid or ashamed, these emotions get in the way of you overcoming obstacles. Either your thoughts or your emotions, or both, can lead you to stop working on your vision. You lose your passion. You become submissive and no longer think about your goals or what's important to you. Your reactions to obstacles stopped you from even trying.

Think about the last obstacle you faced. What thoughts did you have? What emotions did you have?

Were your reactions to the last obstacle you faced accurate? Were they helpful? What is your pattern of responding to obstacles?

The truth is that achieving most goals means overcoming obstacles. That's normal and part of the process. IT'S A PART OF THE PROCESS, PEOPLE. There's a quote from Frank Clark that I enjoy: "If you find a path with no obstacles, it probably doesn't lead anywhere." I believe obstacles can be overcome and that, sometimes, you have to pivot. Sometimes, you have to work around them or find alternatives. This is what pivoting looks like. The key is not to give up because you hit an obstacle or because of your emotional reaction to the obstacle. Just place one foot solid on the ground and pivot. Find a way or make away.

The ability to pivot is why education and exposure are so important. If the power goes out in your house, but you have a generator, most adults know that they can use that generator to create power. Most children do not know what a generator is, or how to operate one. As a result, when the power goes out and a child is home alone, they do not know of any other options, even if there is a generator there, and they simply accept the fact that they have to walk around in darkness. The same goes for the obstacles you face in daily life, big and small. When you are exposed to more and know more, you have more options to pivot. You know how to do more with what is around you and how to roll with the punches.

One thing we say in my household is that you can only control what you can control. The biggest thing you can control is how much you know, your level of education. I had to know that it was even possible for an ordinary person to buy a vending machine before that was an option.

I had to know how to use the vending machine money to flip houses in real estate. If I had not taken the time to learn any of this, I would still be operating in debt today, instead of being free from it. I would not have known of any uses of my bonus money besides paying bills and Christmas shopping. You have to take the time to learn. It's a great thing you picked up this book.

Back to the art of the pivot. As I touched on earlier, it's important that you focus on and keep your vision in mind. This is because some pivots are more intensive and take longer than others. You may get inspired by this book and quit your job tomorrow (which I wholeheartedly do not advise). Then, after a couple weeks, you realize starting a business isn't as easy as you thought and that you probably will not be on *Shark Tank* within your first three weeks of operation. Pivot. Get another job. When starting out, many people need a bridge job. The difference is that you are working that job with the intention of furthering your own agenda and laboring toward your own vision. You are no longer working for a paycheck simply to subsist. You are working for the means that will allow you to survive while you are building something greater. That may sound like a lot of work. Well, it is. My husband and I spent YEARS working a job while we were building; we'd come home after work, deal with our kids, and then stay up until the wee hours of the morning working on our businesses. Like I said before, you have to be willing to do today what others won't, so that you can accomplish tomorrow what others can't.

Now, I want to get back to the founders of Airbnb. When they initially decided to make this quick pivot, they had to recognize the opportunity available to them. There are special points in time where opportunities are made available to you. Because they were ready to pivot when they needed to, and they had the knowledge and exposure to take advantage of a dispensation in time, Brian Chesky and his team took advantage of an opportunity. Their opportunity was hidden in that point in time; they just had to RECOGNIZE IT.

Some of these opportunities will come a lot more literally than the ones discussed here. Sometimes, people will explicitly offer to help you, but somehow people muster up the nerve to ignore them or turn a blind eye. Whenever I have encountered someone who is where I want to be, I do everything in my power to make myself available to learn from them. I've missed birthdays, social gatherings, and other things that are important to me because the value of their teachings is apparent, and I would be foolish not to take advantage of them. You have to be an agent in your own rescue, and when people go out of their way to help you, the least you can do is step up to the plate and answer the call. There are so many people who have asked me for help. I take time out of my day to schedule a call, and then they don't pick up. I tell you I can introduce you to someone who will open doors for you in your field and have a dramatic impact on the dreams that you wish to make a reality in your life, and you're late? You're forsaking opportunities that God is giving you. Recognize them for the life-changing opportunities that they are.

Once you identify a valuable opportunity and decide to take advantage of it, the next step that is of the utmost importance is focus. The action word FOCUS means to intentionally align your mental, physical, and emotional efforts toward a singular goal. While that goal may involve multiple tasks, all of those tasks are centered around a singular desired outcome: for you to effectively leverage that opportunity in a way that gets you further to your vision, goals, and destiny. After I enrolled in Marshawn Evans's mastermind group, everything I did was centered around the idea of me becoming a force to change the financial blueprint of women of color just like me. I tirelessly worked with this end in mind, and I did not let temptation or distraction lead me off course.

Opportunity is the doorway. Be intentional about focusing. Intentional focus is the determination necessary to travel through that doorway in a path aimed singularly toward what it is that you desire on the other side. Any opportunity may open the door to many things, and many of them may seem more enticing than the reason you seized the opportunity in the first place. But they are not in line with your passion, they will not leave you fulfilled, and you won't bring as much value to as many people as you would have if you had stuck with your vision. Therefore, it follows that you most likely will not make as much money because, as we now know, wealth is a by-product of providing the most utility you can to the greatest number of people possible.

Take the Airbnb founders once again. They started a novelty cereal company that they used to help finance the debt for Airbnb. Imagine if they had gotten comfortable and lost sight of their true goal? On the path to your destiny, there will be many rough patches, uncomfortable places that you will have to grind to get out of. But sometimes the places that are even harder to get out of are the comfortable places. When you're running, sprinting relentlessly along the path your vision takes you, you might start to feel the grass get soft beneath your feet. You look up and the sun is shining, the temperature is perfect, there are steaks on the grill, crabs by the bushel... Wait, where was I? Oh, yeah—while pursuing your vision, there will be temptations for you to stop and stay somewhere comfortable.

The Airbnb founders could have said, "Hey, no one likes our idea. Everyone thinks we're crazy, and frankly, we're tired of putting in all this work and getting laughed out of every investment pitch. We seem to be pretty good at making novelty cereal, though. Developing a completely new app and introducing a concept that is foreign and uncomfortable to most people could take years to catch on, whereas everyone likes cereal. Why don't we just take our shoes off, rest here for a while, and see where this road takes us?" That, my friends, is a lack of focus.

Those who are serious about accomplishing their lifelong dreams pursue them despite any positive or negative temptations that come their way to steer them off course. They do this by constantly reminding themselves of their ultimate vision. That is why my advice to you is to write your vision down. Be descriptive and precise. Then, keep it on you or by you so that you see it at least once every day. Put it on a big piece of paper in huge font and tape it to your ceiling so that it's the first thing you see when you wake up in the morning and the last thing you see when you got to sleep at night. Carry it around on a piece of paper folded in your wallet so that while you're on your elevator ride up to your 9-5, you can remember that the only reason you're still working it is to allow you the luxury to go home and pursue your passion on your own time.

If the Airbnb founders had gotten complacent and had abandoned their original dream, they would have missed out on what has grown to be an industry-disrupting service and application. Airbnb has been raising cash at a $30 billion valuation. You know how much novelty cereal you would've had to sell to reach that? We are talking oceans full of Obama O's. Do not settle for what seems like a lot now but what pales in comparison to what you could achieve if you maintain focus.

To sum it all up, you must be ready to act and take advantage of the opportunities life presents to you. Some will be easier to identify than others, but if you snatch up enough of them (and the correct ones, not just any old scheme that comes along), you will begin to see your life change as you strategically pursue opportunities that fall in line with and resonate with your giver's calling. You must also recognize when it is necessary for you to pivot. The time you spend continuing to do things in an unprofitable way simply because you are accustomed to it, the less time you can devote to trying new methods, avenues, or blueprints that are more adaptable to the consumer's demands or market trends. Then, after you identify an opportunity and pivot to create new opportunity, you must keep your focus on your long-term vision at all times. Every move I make—whether it is an email blast, a conference, or a Facebook live stream—it is with the end goal in mind of changing the financial blueprints of millions of people of all races and creeds across the globe.

When I talk about intentional focus, I'm talking about having the ability and the singleness of thought and discipline to agree only to the most important thing at this moment and to disagree with and say no to everything else. I believe that intentional focus is the invisible life force or superpower behind every decision we make to build wealth and the choices we make on this journey. You have to be able to focus to gain clarity.

If you ever want to achieve astonishing outcomes, then you have to start from the core source of all your desires, decisions, choices, emotions, feelings, and experiences, which is your intentional focus. To focus requires us to use our imaginations to empower us to give us our expected outcomes. A major part of our population believes that we are continuously driving in the direction of what we focus on, when the truth is, because of bad past programming, we don't have the right kind of focus at all. Our programming has involuntarily lead us to focus our time and thoughts dwelling on the roots of fear and on all that we don't want, are not qualified for, our educational inabilities, or what we fear will happen if we try. By allowing ourselves to imagine or involuntarily feel negative outcomes, we inform our minds to prepare for what we don't want instead of intentionally focusing on what's possible or focusing on seeing massive opportunities. I remember reading once that Tony Robbins said, "The first force that truly controls our life is the primary decision of Focus."

Millions of people are clueless of the gigantic capacity we can instantly command when we focus all of our mental resources on cultivating and mastering one single area of our lives. Take an audit on what you tend to give your attention to the most. What are you inclined to focus on the most? Are these the areas of your life that you can control or the areas of your life you have no control over, like inflation or taxes? Do you focus on the things you have in your human asset inventory, like your talents, your abilities, and your gifts, or do you focus on all the things that are absent from your life? Do you focus on the past or the present? Do you give thought to the future and plan accordingly? If you are honest with yourself and you dig deep for the answers to the previous questions I asked you, then the answers to these questions will reveal to you your true pattern of focus.

You can't change the way you live until you change the way you think, and before you can form a new way of thinking, you need to give much thought and attention to the direction of your focus, what emotions this brings up for you, and what choices you are making that are in direct correlation with your focus.

I don't think people understand the power of their decisions. We all have been given the ability to make decisions. Out of all of God's creations, its man to which He gave the ability to decide and make conscious choices. By comprehending the few essential decisions that everyone makes on a daily basis, we give ourselves permission to empower and enlarge our territories or to shrink back from who we were created to be and to get off-track—all based on the decisions we make. We have to develop the skill of harnessing the superpower of focus.

So, in building wealth, you have to decide on what's worthy of your focus?

- Essential Decision #1: What are you committed to focus on?
- Essential Decision #2: What are you willing to give up so you can focus?
- Essential Decision #3: What are the action steps you need to take to focus?

I remember when my youngest son, who plays football at Penn State University, wanted to start in his position. The minute he decided to focus,

I asked him what his plan was for the summer. Because he had grown up in a home where vision and intentional focus were taught, he was prepared to answer me. He knew he had to create the time in his schedule to catch 8,000 balls during his off-season to become what he wanted to be. He knew that desire alone wasn't enough. You need to be intentional about your focus.

CHAPTER 10

Financial Discovery & Control

A mentor once asked me, "How would your life change if your annual income became your monthly income?" I was speechless. The question stopped me dead in my tracks. Do you know how difficult it was for me to grasp that mentally? I didn't think about anything else for the rest of the day. No one had ever asked me that question before. I didn't even know that it was possible at the time. Now that I've done business deals that have TRIPLED my annual income in ONE DAY and with one transaction, I know that it's possible. But if my mentor had never asked me that question, I would have never known that I could do that. Imagine that: your annual income becoming your monthly income! How about this? Imagine your annual income becoming your daily income! How would that change your life? What would that look like for you? You have to design your financial future on purpose. Nothing just happens.

What from your experience tells you that you can't change that number? See, when I posed that question, what did your mindset think at that moment? What were you thinking when you read that? Like, right now... I want you to take a moment and think about that. Write it down in the margin of this book.

Now, what comes to mind as to why this may not be possible for you? The thoughts that you may have had at that moment are only indicators of your money mindset. They are NOT THE REAL ISSUES. When I ask this question to my clients, I get responses like these:

1. The economy is bad; no one is building wealth.
2. I don't have access to the right people to make it happen.

3. I don't have the time to do it.
4. I don't have the right support system.
5. I have low self-esteem.
6. I always put other people first and don't have time to do anything for myself.
7. Who's going to help me make this happen?
8. I have small children, and I don't have time.
9. I don't have the money.
10. I'm not a go-getter like you.

All of these are excuses, and they're just signs or indicators of financial mindset issues. These things are not the real issue. You are looking in the wrong place.

What is the highest annual income that you've ever made in your life? Think about it. I want you to write that number down in the margins of this book or somewhere else. Then, I want you to answer this question: How would your life change if you made your annual income your monthly income? What would you do? Would you...

- Travel more?
- Pay your kids' college tuition in full, years ahead of schedule?
- Put $20,000+ away monthly for your retirement?
- Purchase a home for your kids (perhaps even paying cash for it)?
- Get a vacation home on several continents?
- Donate to organizations you care about?
- Retire your parents?
- Retire your siblings?
- Build schools in underdeveloped countries?

You have to think about, and have a plan for, your money. What will you do, when it comes? It's about getting in position to attract wealth in your life. When it comes, what will you do with it? Do you even know?

This reminds me of a true story. I got a telephone call a couple of years ago from my pastor, who wanted me to talk to another pastor who had an NFL player as a part of his ministry. The guy had just been drafted and had received a huge signing bonus and now had the highest salary that he had ever made in his life. He wanted to give the whole signing bonus to the ministry. The pastor called me because, for years, they had believed that someone would put a lot of money into the ministry because they were doing a lot of things. They were helping people in Haiti, and just doing a lot of different things in the ministry. He called because, even though he had been hoping for this kind of money for a long time, now that it was available, he didn't know what to do with it.

Listen, if you believe that more abundance will come in your life, you've got to have a plan for it when it gets there. You've got to know what you want to do with it. There's no reason for you believing that all of these things will happen in your life if you don't have a plan for it, if you don't know what you're going to do with it when it gets there. Because guess what? It's not going to happen. Money is attracted to those who know what to do with it.

How would your life change if you made your annual income your monthly income? What would you do?

See, personal success = human potential. It takes GROWTH to step into it. It takes you being in control of your money and not your money controlling you. There are a couple of questions which you must be able to answer in this regard.

1. Are you WILLING to do whatever is required to get the manifestation that you desire?

2. Are you ABLE? Can you see in your mind the things that you want to experience in the physical realm?

What is your GODCLASS VISION for your finances and for your life? I want you to write it down. What do you really want? WHO DO YOU NEED TO BECOME TO GET THERE? That's really important. Most people don't know who they need to BE to gain financial freedom, and they are unaware of what they need to focus on to get there. You need to know your financial freedom number. You can't have a complete plan without knowing your desired destination. See, just getting out of debt is not the completion of a financial freedom plan. There is more to the equation.

Ask yourself how much money you need to make to live the lifestyle you want. I'm going to say that again. Ask yourself how much money you need to make to live the lifestyle you want. Don't just throw a number out there. Actually give it some thought.

We have already taken the time to note all of your expenses. Remember, finances have a buildable blueprint model. That's the importance of having a money coach—you need to have someone who has already gone through the process, who can show you an accelerated path to follow, and who can help you build from the right foundation.

What is your Financial Freedom Number?

In order for you to know your financial freedom number, you have to combine your annual expenses with the cost of your dreams, and then divide that by 12. That's the monthly income that you need. This becomes part of your strategic money vision board. Remember, I said pretty pictures on poster board don't give you a strategic plan. This is your strategic plan. You have to get started on your wealth plan. In fact, you've already taken the first steps to your wealth journey by reading this book.

STEP ONE is to add up all of your known annual expenses and bills, which you have done. (At least I'm hoping you've done that by now. If you haven't, go back to Chapter 8 and do it now.)

STEP TWO in the Personal Currency Mapping process is to ADD NEW PURCHASES that you want to make over the next 12 months. Be very specific and clear about this.

STEP THREE to the Personal Currency Mapping process is to ADD TAXES, INSURANCE PAYMENTS, HEALTH CARE COSTS, AND EVERY OTHER EXPENSE.

STEP FOUR to the Personal Currency Mapping process is to DIVIDE THE TOTAL NUMBER BY 12 to get you your monthly MUST MOVE TO EMPOWER EQUATION!

This gives legs to your compelling "WHY." See, I often say that when your "WHY" is big enough, your "how" becomes easy. My "WHY" in the beginning was that I didn't want my children to start from ground zero. I wanted to be able to give my children an advantage in life, and I wanted to expose them to something that was greater than the local area that we lived in. They were my "WHY." I didn't want my kids to go to college and have to spend the next 16 years paying off their student loans. I didn't want my children to be in a situation where there was more month than money. I knew that whatever I didn't change, my children were going to repeat.

If I hadn't decided that I didn't want to live like that anymore, nothing would have changed. See, that's why I call this my MUST MOVE TO EMPOWER EQUATION NUMBER. This gives legs to your compelling "WHY." You have to come up with a great enough "WHY." What is your "WHY"? What would get you to move when you don't feel like moving? What would get you to move when you become discouraged because the process isn't going fast enough? You have to keep your "WHY" with you.

See, the word *empower* means to authorize. It means to qualify, to equip. Knowing this number, this information lets you know WHY you are even in the game of money and why you are playing this game to win. It gives you control over your financial future.

Every week, when my son has a football game, the team comes together to watch film on the opposing team. They watch the film so they can learn what sorts of things the other team does based on their formation. They watch to become familiar with the opponent and the type of game they will be playing. Next, they watch film to observe key players, and then they look for different signals that the key players make. It helps them with their game plan. It helps them with their playbook. See, your opponent in this game is debt. Your opponent in this game is a bad money blueprint. Your opponent in this game is inflation and taxes. You are the key player in this game, and your current money blueprint and scoreboard are the signals you should be looking for.

Again, knowing this number, your MUST MOVE TO EMPOWER EQUATION, gives you a visual of what you are moving towards. Knowing this number allows you to understand your game plan and to see opportunities that make you a winner in this game. You're no longer playing the money game to lose; you're playing to win. This number is your DESTINATION, your purpose point. This number will provide the life you dream of and plan for!

A destination is a place where someone is going or a place where someone is being sent. Many people lack a set destination for their money. I call it DESTINATION WEALTH. Most people don't have a clear plan on how to get there. When the cash flow from your businesses and investments are greater than your monthly living expenses, then you've reached financial freedom. I knew that if my monthly expenses were

$12,000 a month, then I needed to generate enough cash flow to be able to handle this.

You can actually start the process with something small, something easy, like your electric bill. If your monthly electric bill is $300 a month, what can you do to currently bring in $300 a month to cover that expense? I'll show you how I take my clients through the process. We are going to pick one or two different expenses that you have. Then, I'm going to teach you how to generate enough money to handle those expenses. The goal is to start creating enough cash flow to take care of each one of your monthly expenses and bills. That's always the goal, guys: to be able to generate enough additional cash flow to take care of one of your expenses. Again, when the cash flow you receive from your businesses and your investments is greater than your monthly living expenses, then you've reached financial freedom.

How much money do you need to make each month to live the life that you want? It's imperative that you know that number. You have to think big. Small thinking and small actions lead to being broke and unfulfilled. When you begin to think big and take massive action steps, you get more money and more meaning in your life.

Don't just guess at a number and pull it blindly out the sky. Take some time to be clear on what the cost of being THE FUTURE YOU will be. Take some time to be clear on what your life costs will be. Add it up so that you can see that the money that you will be making actually means something to you.

When I started, I knew that sending my kids to independent schools, or sending them to some of the best schools in the country, wasn't an option for me. It was something I HAD to do. I also knew that my earned income alone wasn't going to cut it, especially if I wanted to maintain my current standard of living. It cost me a little over $98,000 a year to send my three kids to independent schools at that time. And that was just elementary and middle school! That didn't even include college tuition. When I tell people that number, they look at me like I'm crazy. It's actually cheaper for me to send my son to college and pay his tuition in full than it was for me to send him to middle school and high school when he was attending an all-boys college preparatory school. Again, cutting that wasn't an option for me. I knew that we simply had to be able to generate enough cash flow to handle this. This number was added to my MUST MOVE TO EMPOWER EQUATION.

You have to include all the things that mean something to you into this equation. I knew I wanted to take at least three vacations a year. I researched the cost of the destinations that I wanted to go to, and I added this number in the equation. My oldest son had been traveling overseas since he was in the 6th grade. One year, he went to seven different European countries. I knew I wanted my kids to have this advantage in life, so I had to add this to my equation.

To arrive at the result of your MUST MOVE TO EMPOWER EQUATION, you have to:

- Add up ALL your known ANNUAL expenses (i.e., all of your monthly bills, plus any quarterly or annual bills).
- Add the specific purchases you want to make over the next 12 months.
- Add the values from the first two steps and divide this sum by 12 to get your MONTHLY FINANCIAL GOAL.

Here are the cold hard facts. Ninety-five percent of Americans are NOT financially free. This is not because they want to stay in debt but because they never decide to be financially free. We've been programmed to believe in the 60+ year JOB (or what I call "Just Over Broke") plan. From the age of five, we are programmed to go to school, learn how to follow instructions and be overloaded with information that we will never need in life; then, we graduate to get a good job and work for someone else the rest of our lives. You end up spending 60+ years of your life working and hopefully saving enough for your retirement. Stats show that more than one-third of all working-age adults have NOT saved for retirement. Almost 70% of Millennials who are out there now have not started saving for retirement, yet the power of compounding interest would make them millionaires if they started early. I want to educate you so you can educate others.

Knowing the rules of money and wealth helps you avoid dependency. The Bible says, in Ecclesiastes 7:12, that money is a defense. It helps you avoid being dependent on your job. It helps you avoid being dependent on the government. It helps you avoid being dependent on anybody. I often tell women that your man should not be your financial plan. Knowing the rules of money and wealth helps you avoid dependency. It helps you avoid dependency on your parents. It helps you know what limits are on your income, how to increase your self-esteem, and how to control your time (that's a big one).

I like waking up when I'm done sleeping. I don't want anybody else controlling my time or telling me when I can go see my kids' games—and when it's something important to them, I need to be present. I don't want to have to ask for permission to take time off. Again, knowing the rules of money and wealth helps you control your time, and it helps you break the glass ceiling of lack and poverty that is above your generation. You will always be dependent until you hold the purse of your own. I'll say that again: You will always be dependent until you hold the purse of your own.

There are a couple of issues with this "institutional programming plan" (as I call it) that our current school system is creating. The first thing is that it takes 60+ years sometimes (researchers say it takes an average of 67 years) to get through the system, and those are the best years of your life. That's the majority of your earning potential years. And the second issue that I have with it is that this 60+ year plan JUST DOESN'T WORK.

About 11 years ago, I was working with a lady who had retired. She had put away $260,000 for her retirement. Because she didn't seek wise counsel before retiring, she made very poor decisions with this money. First, she elected to take it up-front and was taxed heavily. Secondly, she decided to purchase a new home when she was in her late 60s and was, therefore, starting all over with a new 30-year mortgage. By the time she came to me and I worked out the numbers, I realized that in eight years, all of that money would have been gone if she didn't make any changes. EIGHT YEARS for $260,000 to be gone! She was on the cusp of outliving her money, and she didn't have a plan for that. That's why you have to look at your money with a long-range view. Guess what? That was 16 years ago. Guess what else? She's working again. You have to be able to prepare for your future.

When you look at the 5% of Americans who become financially free and financially independent, you should ask yourself, "What did they do to achieve financial freedom?" In most cases, they achieved their financial freedom by creating business systems. They became business owners and focused on building a sustainable, successful business. YOU WILL NEVER BECOME WEALTHY OR GAIN FREEDOM FROM EARNED INCOME ALONE. I don't care how large your salary is. I have clients who make extravagant incomes, and they are not financially independent or financially free. The main reason for this is that they live off 100% of their earned income. Wealth and entrepreneurship really are about having the ability to buy back your time. As I've said before, true wealth is measured in time and not in money. It's about how long you can maintain your standard of living without working. When you earn a high salary, it's not for nothing. To much is given, much is required. You will spend the majority of your time traveling for the benefit of the corporation that is paying you that high salary. You will miss valuable moments with your family and friends if this is your only source of income.

Building a business is the OFFENSIVE PLAYBOOK STRATEGY in your financial playbook. Creating cash flow streams will increase your income and accelerate your journey to financial freedom. Remember, when we worked towards creating a currency surplus (which you SHOULD be putting into your Golden Goose Account—a.k.a., your Financial Freedom Account), it was said that the purpose of creating this surplus is to assist you in funding your new business endeavor. Yes, just managing your money can set you free, but it will take you a long time.

Most of us are not patient. Obviously, millions of Americans are not patient. This is one of the reasons that budgets don't work. Budgets don't incorporate a wealth expansion plan. Budgets don't teach you how to expand your means. They only teach you how to live below your means. Living below your means, or even within your means, doesn't create multiple streams of income. If what you have right now isn't enough, creating a budgeting plan doesn't magically make it more than enough. Budgeting doesn't multiply your money. Ultimately, people want two things: more time and more money. Creating multiple streams of income actually gives that to you. It gives you more time and more money.

I've mentioned this previously, but it is relevant to this discussion as well: When I hit the stage and speak all over the country, one of the first things I ask is, "How many of you would like a little bit more money?"

Almost every single time, 100% of the people in the room raise their hand. When I talk about creating cash flow and building "sustainable cash flow cows" (as my business partner calls them), I mean the type of business that will eventually run on its own without your day-to-day involvement. Another way of putting it, if someone has to show up for work every day, it won't be you.

Most businesses fail because they lack systemization. Another thing I've mentioned earlier which bears repeating here is something that my mentor always used to tell me: "Systems set you free." Creating systems that handle your money and your business is a part of the ultimate successful financial plan. Constant current cash flow: That's what a cash cow is.

Earned Income alone keeps you DEPENDENT. If you are only an employee, you are dependent because your income is dependent on someone else (your employer). You have no control over your own well-being. If it's no longer financially feasible for the company to keep you, guess what? They won't. If it makes financial sense for your employer to replace you with a robot, guess what? They will! It doesn't matter how long or how hard you've worked for them. It doesn't matter if you have a great relationship with your boss or not. The truth of the matter is, when you have to go, you're gone.

We are seeing this in 2019. Many people learned this by force a few years ago when the government shut down. A long time ago, I decided that I would not leave my financial future in the hands of a crazy boss. That just wasn't going to happen to me. I was not going to leave my financial future—or whether my kids were going to have a great Christmas or a great year, or whether they could do the things that they want to do in life—in the hands of my boss. I didn't want these things to depend on whether my boss decided I deserved a raise or a bonus. I am never giving anybody that much power over my finances. That was my decision.

DEPENDENT people include employees, disability recipients, and welfare beneficiaries. INDEPENDENT people include small business owners and private practice professionals (e.g., lawyers, accountants, CPAs, doctors, chiropractors, consultants, etc.)

Being independent means that you are typically self-employed and are not held prey to one client, but you have multiple clients. But even these people really don't have true leverage. Why do I say this? See, not all business enterprises are the same. Remember, the goal is financial FREEDOM. True wealth is measured in time, not in money. Creating cash flow, or creating a cash cow, is about buying back your time. That's essentially what entrepreneurs do. Entrepreneurs set out to buy back their time. Very few of the professionals that I listed earlier have true leverage.

Financial leverage is simply the ability to do more with less. The reason I say this is because the professionals listed above only get paid when THEY do the work. They can't lay on the beaches of Bora Bora and continue to get paid for long periods of time. Take a hair stylist, for instance. A hair stylist can go on vacation whenever they like, but they are limited as to how long they can actually stay on vacation. If they're not doing hair, then they're not making money. The same thing goes for a doctor. I have several friends who are medical doctors. They go on vacation, but they can't stay very long because they don't see any patients while on vacation. And if they don't see any patients, they don't get paid. Even being independent has an aspect of dependency tied to it.

See, with a better understanding of the game of money, you have more control. Then, the greater control that you have, the greater responsibility you have over the amount of money you can make and your financial future. The real voyage of financial discovery consists not of seeking new landscapes for your money but of having new eyes—eyes that see opportunities. That's why I took you on that journey of getting to know your money and identifying your position in the game. What's the financial compass of your money? It's very important that you know where you are because, as I said, the real voyage of financial discovery consists not of seeking new landscapes for your money but of having new eyes. You have to be in the right position to see the right things.

Recently, I had a conversation with my pastor, and he said something that stuck with me. He said, "People want wealth, but they want it like welfare. They don't want to do anything for it." Selah!

My Money Made EASY Masterclass was designed to give you a winning playbook. The ULTIMATE Wealth Plan is a template that the wealthy use all over the globe, and I want to give it to you. It's designed to give you this strategy. There are three steps to it:

1. Start a business.
2. Invest the cash flow from the business into real estate.

3. Invest your excess cash flow into things that compound at a high rate (e.g., paper assets, commodities, cryptocurrency, etc.).

The whole purpose of discovering the cash flow patterns of your money is to allow you to shift its direction. Money becomes easy in this format. It becomes hard when you attempt to build wealth out of order or from a place where your mindset is not set for success (i.e., when you have debt and lack a strategic wealth plan). Money becomes easy when you know what to do.

As long as your money is caught up at the mall; in exchanging places with depreciating cars; and keeping company with MasterCard, Visa, and Discover, and consumer debt, it will never make it to the sandboxes of the seven-figure club. It's as simple as that. EVERYTHING IN THE GAME OF MONEY IS ABOUT POSITIONING. EVERYTHING IS ABOUT BUILDING THE BLOCKS NEEDED TO CONSTRUCT A STRONG WEALTH FOUNDATION. If you never change your mindset, you will never have the willpower to create a surplus with your money. My grandfather taught me, "Always have something left over."

The mission is to create WEALTH, not WANTS. That's what a surplus is. A surplus has a mission. Money has a mission, and the mission is to create wealth, not want. Money in the hands of the poor creates more wants, not more wealth. We are building your financial house one block at a time. Most people lack the knowledge and the structure of having a wealth plan. That's why they get frustrated working a job all their life and remaining in financial bondage.

Wealth has ACCELERATORS, and the Ultimate Wealth Plan is one such accelerator. Accelerators speed up the process. If you want financial freedom, whatever that number was that we just calculated, starting a business is an accelerator. Investing that into real estate is an accelerator. Investing that into cash flow and then into paper assets is an accelerator. It speeds up the process so you can live a freedom-based lifestyle. Wealth is a lifestyle.

People who don't have a wealth coach, who try to do it on their own, have uninformed plans that look like this:

- They deposit their money into a savings account (I'm not talking about their Golden Goose Account, either).
- They just want to get out of debt.
- They buy a personal residence.
- They put their money in mutual funds.
- They dibble and dabble in little stocks.
- They might have 401(K)s and IRAs.

NONE OF THESE ARE ACCELERATORS. All of these things are part of a weak plan and make for a very long route to financial freedom. But that's all that most Americans know how to do: Have a little savings, get out of debt, maybe buy a house, get some mutual funds or a 401k plan, and then that's it. That plan doesn't have any of the accelerators that you need to build a wealthy lifestyle.

Asset Classes

ACCELERATORS are legal instruments that add VELOCITY to your wealth plan. Velocity is momentum. It's speed. It's one of the things that you need to implement in your life that will give your money momentum, that will give your money velocity, that will speed up your process for financial freedom. The Ultimate Wealth Plan includes assets and accelerators. Listen closely, because this is what I call the Money School part of this book. You need to know the various asset classes, which are as follows:

1. Business systems
2. Real estate
3. Paper assets (stocks, bonds, mutual funds, etc.)
4. Commodities (I refer to anything that comes from the Earth that you can invest in as a commodity. These include things like gas, oil, silver, gold, water, precious metals and semi-precious stones, and even wind – you can invest in wind technology right now.)

For the sake of time and to prevent this chapter from being way too long, I am going to deal with only three areas: business systems, real estate, and paper assets.

1. Business Systems – I love the ability to multiply my money through business enterprises. When you own your own business, if you are successful at it, it can generate the most income of all your income streams with the least amount of work and with the least taxes paid. Tax codes were written to favor business owners. The government rewards you in the tax codes for doing two things: providing affordable housing for the public and creating jobs.

One of the things I love to do in my spare time is to research the movement of currency with billionaires because they are the ones who set the tone for global wealth trends. Years ago, I learned that one of the reasons that Warren Buffet turned his company, Berkshire Hathaway, into an insurance company and not a clothes manufacturing company or a garment manufacturing company is that the tax advantages of an insurance company are significantly greater.

The tax rules are different for different businesses. This is important because taxes are your single LARGEST expense. One of the things that I do when I vacation is to research the vacation spots of billionaires, and then I learn why they go there. For instance, a couple years ago, my kids wanted to go to Bermuda. So, before we went, I researched who lives in Bermuda, who owns property in Bermuda, and who does business in Bermuda. I learned that Edward Johnson (the founder of Fidelity Investments) owns homes in Bermuda. I learned that Carlos Slim Helu, who is the wealthiest man in the world (he's actually Mexican) owns properties and homes in Bermuda. Warren Buffett, John Fredrickson, Ross Perot, Ronald Lauder— they all own homes in Bermuda. When I started doing my research, I learned that this is because Bermuda is a tax shelter for real estate.

Again, it's all about knowing what to do with your money and being smart with it. Even in business, it's so much more than just saying, "I have my own business." It's learning about what the right kinds of businesses to have are and which businesses involve tax shelters so that you can actually hedge yourself against inflation, tax increases, and debt.

There are several accelerators at your disposal if you own a business. One accelerator in particular that I want to talk about is using OPM (other people's money). Micro-loans and using companies like Kickstarter.

com, Crowdfunding, Fundrazr, RocketHub, Pozible, Fundable, Ulule, and Fundanything.com are methods people are currently using in the new economy to get around the strict guidelines of the banking industry since the last market meltdown in 2008/2009. Using OPM gives you leverage. And banks only fund 15% of "A" credit borrowers.

I don't believe that all debt is bad debt. When Rob and I first started out in the real estate market years ago, we borrowed money to buy properties. We made about $47,000 off of the first house that we bought, fixed up, and sold, and that one transaction paid off all of our consumer debt, including the debt of the loan we took out to buy the house. That's why I don't believe that all debt is bad debt. If that were true, then the Bible wouldn't have told the Israelites to go borrow from their neighbors when they were getting ready to leave captivity. That was a version of OPM. I used OPM to get started in my real estate business, and it paid off.

Choosing the right format for your business is another accelerator. If you are thinking about starting a business, you need to decide whether your goal is to grow a limited liability company (LLC), S-corp, C-corp, sole proprietorship, general partnerships, or limited partnership (LPs). Learning what type of business you should have is extremely important. You also have to learn which states you can incorporate your business in such that your tax liability and personal assets liability are minimized. One of my favorite states to incorporate in is Nevada because there are no corporate taxes or information sharing there, and the HOLDER of bare sharers is protected. Know why you're incorporating and what state you're incorporating in.

Deciding the right corporate structure in which to house your business is CRITICAL. Sole proprietorships and general partnerships are two of the worst business formations you can choose. There is absolutely NO asset protection under these formations, and owning a business is all about asset protection. You need to understand the pros and cons of each and decide what's best for your company. Know the benefits and the requirements of each. You need to know which entity will provide the best protection for your business and result in the best tax advantages, thus maximizing your cash flow. A book that I recommend to everyone is called *Inc. and Grow Rich* (Inc. as in Incorporate). It's not the same as *Think and Grow Rich*.

It's "Inc." I-N-C. *Inc. and Grow Rich.* This will educate you on different business structures and why it's best to incorporate in certain states.

Just as you can take advantage of OPM as an accelerator, you can also use OPT (other people's time). If you are a smart business owner and are excellent at what you do, then leveraging other people and systems will help you accelerate your operations. Most people will have to work for money for much of their lives because they are working FOR a business rather than working to BUILD a business. There is a difference between the two.

In my brokerage firm, we use virtual assistants for absolutely everything. Why? Because I don't want to sit on the phone making cold calls all day. I can pay somebody else to do that. Learning how to leverage OPT is one of the ways that makes your business successful and helps set up systems.

Moreover, learning about and taking advantage of tax laws is an accelerator that business owners use. See, tax codes were written for business owners and investors. Uncle Sam loves you if you are a business owner. By starting a business, you may be able to convert personal expenses into legitimate deductible business expenses.

Even giving to charity is a type of accelerator. Being a generous giver and giving back to your community are essential elements to growing your business. The IRS rewards you for being a giver, and so does God.

2. Real Estate – You will be hard-pressed to find a wealthy person who does not have real estate in their portfolio of assets and investments. Real estate is an accelerator. Again, we use real estate to accelerate our path. Even in our business, it was buildable for us. We owned vending machines before we owned real estate. The money—the surplus—that we got from the vending machines gave us the money we needed to buy real estate. The surplus that we got from real estate gave us the ability to buy our brokerage firm. And the surplus from the brokerage firm has allowed us to be private lenders. Now, I'm no longer confessing the scripture: I literally am a lender and not a borrower. Everything is a buildable process.

Even with real estate, you have to understand the difference between capital gains and cash flow. I remember when we first started out, I had gone flipping happy. I was buying, fixing up, and flipping everything. At that time, my real estate coach called me on the phone, and she said, "LaShawne, it is time for you to stop flipping. There's a difference between cash flow and capital gains." When you invest for capital gains, you end up paying more in taxes. The way you set up your income for a lifetime through real estate is by buying properties and getting renters in there because, remember, you are trying to get enough cash flow to cover your expenses and the cost of the future you. If I have five rental income units, and those five rental income units can replace my earned income for paying for my monthly expenses and bills, I've achieved my goal. Again (and maybe real estate is not your thing), I'm just letting you know that you'll be hard-pressed to find any multimillionaire or successful business person who does not have any real estate holdings.

Some of the specific accelerators we discussed for businesses also apply to real estate. The first is OPM. Money borrowed as unsecured loans or contributed by a small group of stockholders (shareholders) are examples of this accelerator.

Selecting the right format (entity) is another accelerator that you should take advantage of. You have to understand corporate structures to understand the secrets and the strategies that wealthy people have used for generations to protect their real estate assets. Many people don't know this. Often, you will want to have separate entities for each property so that if one property is put at risk, the others are not. Popular corporate structures for real estate holdings are LLCs and LPs. Find a competent real estate attorney or a tax strategist because you may end up basing your decisions on really important state-specific laws.

Finally, the tax codes offer awesome accelerators to your real estate income and cash flow in the form of depreciation, also known in the real estate world as phantom cash flow, which means more money flows into the investor's pocket today and not when they retire.

3. Paper Assets – NOTE: The investments of wealthy people are very different from the investments of regular retail investors. Regular retail investors are the people I call who will meet with people from American Express, Fidelity, or New York Mutual. They are actually quite like salespeople and cannot teach you any type of investment education. With paper assets, you have to know the difference between a salesperson and a true investment educator. When I talk about retail investors, I mean people who call up a certified financial planner. That's not where the real money is.

This is merely for informational purposes and to give you a general knowledge of investment terms to familiarize yourself with the new language of money that you're going to be using. The average person, when you talk about investing, automatically thinks about mutual funds, 401Ks, and IRAs. But wealthy people play in a different investment sandbox. Literally, there are conferences that I have access to now for which your net worth has to be a certain amount before you are allowed in. But the things that they are investing in will blow your mind. The investment strategies that they use are incredible, and that's why it's important for you to know the cycles of investing, which is something that I teach every year at my live event, Wealthy Women Rock, which you have access to.

My pastor always used to tell me that you plan a company for where you're going, not for where you're currently operating. I absorbed this information years ago, and it's how I planned my wealth playbook. Let me now introduce you to a few accelerators that are available to investors.

The first is tax exemption. Uncle Sam offers even greater leveraged advantages to investors who invest in projects the government needs financial assistance with, like REITs (real estate investment trusts). The government gives you different tax advantages for investing in those things.

Hedge Funds are another great accelerator. These are really risky and largely unregulated US investment partnerships which really employ aggressive leverage to multiple gains. They are restricted to 100 people or less, and you have to have a minimum of $1 million to invest. But, recalling my earlier recommendation that you should start reading financial magazines, it is important to know what a hedge fund is now even if you have nowhere near $1 million to invest. You don't know who's going to come across your path, who you may get into the elevator with one day when you do have a lot of money to invest. I will tell you, the Bible says, "No one listens to a poor man." You need to be able to hold a conversation with wealthy people because they have a different language. I thought it was really important that I give you a general working knowledge of some of these terms. For wealthy people, hedge funds allow you to invest with insurance.

Options are something that I dabble in. The benefit of an option is when a company allows an employee to buy stock in the company at a discounted rate or a stated fixed price.

PPMs (private placement memorandums) are private placement offerings of stock in a company that is exempt from federal regulations.

One of my favorite accelerators that I've been able to build wealth with are IPOs (initial public offerings). IPOs are the first offerings of a firm's stock shares on the stock market once it goes public. IPOs present an opportunity for the founders and other investors to make high profits by cashing in on their stock holdings. For instance, when Facebook first went public, I was able to get in on the IPO. That's not the first time, though. I've done a few IPOs over the years.

Awareness is Your Ignition

See, a tough economy just means you have to get smarter in the game of money. Your grandma's piggy bank knowledge won't cut it in today's economy.

Motivation, or your truest "WHY," is the accelerator to your financial dreams. Most people who have their ideas manifest are stuck at the point of motivation. It's easy to say, "I want to fix my money," or "I have an idea." Everybody gets ideas. But *expectation* is an action word. Expectation is something that you do. Expectation means you are actually in action. You have to be in action in order to shift your money blueprint. Being in a tough economy, again, just means that you have to get smarter in the game of money. Creating a business system is what accelerates your path to financial freedom and financial independence.

Dedicate at least one hour a day—consistently, not sometimes—to taking action, to learning about starting a business. Go online, visit bookstores, gather as much information as you can about the industry that you want to be in. If you don't have a clue what kind of business you want to start, think about some of the things people compliment you on the most. What are some of the things that you absolutely love doing?

I often ask people, "What do you have in your hand?" I often share the story from 1 Kings 17 where I first discovered this concept I teach when I'm on stages and in my Born to Multiply Masterclass. In this passage, Elijah met a widow who had given up on life. She was going to just take the little bit of oil she had left and some flour, bake a cake, eat it, and die. It was all she thought she had left (in other words, she couldn't see her opportunity). Elijah told her to go borrow a lot of vessels from her neighbors. She obeyed, and the oil flowed until she ran out of vessels to pour it into. The oil flowed based on her CAPACITY to receive. The prophet asked her "WHAT DO YOU HAVE IN YOUR HAND?" Start with where you are. What do you have in your hand right now? I want you to give some thought to that.

If you have a business already, how do you become THE expert in your industry? Think of ways to increase your value in the marketplace. You get paid based on the value you provide in the marketplace. So, if you render little value, you get paid little money. If you render great value, you get paid great money.

There are certain books that I think that everyone should have:
1. *Think & Grow Rich*, by Napoleon Hill
2. *The BIG Idea*, by Donny Deutsch
3. *Prepare to be a Millionaire*, by Tom Spinks, Kimberly Spinks, and Lindsey Spinks
4. *Outliers*, by Malcolm Gladwell
5. *E-Myth Enterprise*, by Michael Gerber
6. *Loopholes of the Rich*, by Robert Kiyosaki
7. *Before You Quit Your Job*, by Robert Kiyosaki
8. *The Richest Man in Babylon*, by George S. Clayton
9. *The Alchemist*, by Paulo Coelho
10. *Start with WHY*, by Simon Sinek

So, moving forward, when I mentioned earlier about looking to build a successful business, there are three positions you can take: dependent, independent, and interdependent. We've already gone over the dependent and independent positions. The INTERDEPENDENT business model is those used by businesses, companies, and entrepreneurs who co-create with someone else in a win-win partnership. Being interdependent is key to successful business and building alliances with the right network of other business owners.

There are several key criteria to look for:

1. When I'm thinking about doing business, it has to be interdependent. That means that there are key people who I know that I may need help

from to be successful. I want my business to be able to run without me being present every single day.

2. The business must ultimately provide me with ongoing and unlimited income. That's another thing that I look at. I get presented with opportunities all the time, and not all business opportunities are great opportunities. You have to know what you're called to do in the marketplace, or you have to have an idea of what you love to do. If I don't love the business idea, I don't do it. For me, business ultimately has to provide ongoing and unlimited income. If I think that there is going to be a limit to the amount of money that I can make, I won't touch the business. The truth of the matter is that without ongoing income, you can never truly be financially free. To have ongoing income means you get paid on a profitable action without having to be there for it. ALL ongoing income business takes a lot of work to start and build but only a little work to maintain. So, make sure you ask yourself, "Does what I am currently doing have unlimited income potential, or is there a cap to what I can make?"

3. Develop a multi-industry (not a single-industry) opportunity. This means that you want your business to do well during good times and to do great during bad times. You want to move with the market and market trends to stay profitable. You want to be profitable NO MATTER WHAT THE ECONOMY DOES. You want to be profitable, period.

4. Find someone with a proven business system in the industry that you desire to be in or that you are already in. It's so much easier to model success than to re-invent the wheel. I'm going to say that again: It's so much easier to model success than to reinvent the wheel.

Your financial success will depend on what you do in your spare time. I rarely watch television. I told you in the module prior to this one that wealthy people don't waste their time watching television. You may work a job by day, but you become wealthy by night when you build your business, your multiple streams of income. If you want financial freedom bad enough, how big is your "Want to"? Are you willing to make it happen? I ask people that all the time. When you work a job, it doesn't prohibit you from becoming successful by night by building your own business.

Change is possible. You need to:

1. Get irritated. Sometimes, you just have to get irritated enough with your current financial blueprint until the pain of remaining the same

outweighs the growing pains of changing. Years ago, I told a story of how I was financially suffocating before I started, even before I had a business. I remember feeling like I was financially suffocating. For me, there was no option but to shift because if I didn't, I felt like I was going to die in the same place I'd always been in.

2. Get motivated. You have to get motivated. Come up with a big "WHY" to change, a strong, compelling reason to change. For me, my kids were my strong, compelling reason to change. I knew that I did not want them to start from ground zero. I did not want them to be brought up in a lifestyle that was limited just because we couldn't afford to do something. I wanted to be able to give them the exposure in life to something that was bigger than the area that we lived in. I wanted to expose them to other cultures and other people. That was really important to me. That was my "WHY." My husband and I are both only children with our moms, so I knew that we eventually might have had to be in a position to take care of our moms.

Financially, I didn't want to be stuck like the majority of today's sandwich generation. I didn't want to be like those who are not only trying to help their kids, raise their kids, send their kids to college but who are also dealing with the high expenses of helping their parents with their medical bills and just the costs in general that arise as your parents get older. I wanted to be prepared for that. I wanted to be able to help other people. You cannot give from an empty cup. I wanted to be able to be a blessing to other people and live a life of significance. You can't do that when your cup is empty. For me, I had to get motivated. In order for you to stay motivated, you will always need a "WHY." You have to have a compelling "WHY." I tell people all the time, when your "WHY" is big enough, the How becomes easy.

3. Get educated. Learning and continuing education are essential to your financial success. Without ongoing education and learning, you will get stuck. Literally, for the past 18 years, I have constantly been educating myself. Every business enterprise that I have, I have one private coach for that particular business, and I'm always in some form of mastermind because I understand that ongoing learning and continuing education is essential for my success. At every new level that you get to, you need a different level of success. There was a time in my life where I needed a

$100,000 coach. Then, I went to a half-million-dollar, and then to my million-dollar coaches. Once you reach a million dollars, you've got to find yet another coach. Two years ago, I had to find some billionaires to coach me to take me to the next level. Again, learning and continuing education are essential for your financial success.

4. Get active. Most people fail here. This is where the rubber meets the road. You have to get active. To gain success in anything, you have to get moving. You have to take action in order for you to change your life, and you have to take massive action and consistent action. It can't be a once-in-a-while type of gig. It doesn't work like that. Complacency and procrastination are habits of poor people. It is a blocker that keeps most people from living their dreams. This is where your programming really kicks in. If you want something different, you have to do something different. I get that sometimes this process takes you out of your comfort zone, but what I need you to realize is that your income zone is directly tied to your comfort zone. In order for you to live the freedom-based lifestyle that you desire, you must stretch your comfort zone. Most people will never break through barriers.

When most people experience fear, they stop. Fear is such a wealth-blocker. Fear blocks most women from reaching financial freedom. Women literally don't confront what they're fearful of. They don't confront what confuses them. That's why I wanted to do the Money Made Easy Masterclass—so that you can confront the areas that keep you stuck. I wanted to take the mystery out of money. I get that sometimes this process can take you out of your comfort zone, but I really want to stress that your income zone is directly tied to your comfort zone. In order for you to live that freedom-based lifestyle I keep talking about, you have to stretch yourself beyond your comfort zone. Most people will never break through the barriers that they have. When most people experience fear, they stop. When you stop, you stay inside your comfort zone. When you stay inside your comfort zone, you stay exactly where you are. There's no new territory inside your comfort zone.

That's why, in the prayer of Jabez, he said, "Look, Lord, expand my territory." He understood that expansion was necessary for him to go where he desired to go. Expansion is on the outside of your comfort zone, not on the inside of your comfort zone. You also need to know what actions to take. Taking the wrong action is just as crippling as inaction. That's why mentors and coaches are so essential. Having a business or wealth coach is like having the ability to compress decades into days; it gives you the ability to learn from other people's experiences in addition to your own. Remember, success leaves clues.

If you want financial freedom, you have to learn that your FINANCIAL PLAYBOOK has to include hedging yourself against inflation. I often say that the three invisible hands that are in your wallet are debt, inflation, and taxes. You may not be able to do much about inflation and taxes, but you sure can do something about debt. So again, those are the three invisible hands that are in your wallet. Your playbook has to hedge your wallet against inflation by creating multiple streams of income. It doesn't matter when people say that gas prices went up, or that food prices went up. Guess what? Just make more money. That's my philosophy. What do I need to do to be able to bring in more to hedge myself against inflation? It's all a matter of how you look at things.

If you listen to the news, it will scare you out of doing anything. Gas prices can go through the roof. That just means that I need to make more. That's why mentors and coaches are so important.

I get people who ask me all the time, "What can I invest in?" And my first question to them is, "Do you have debt?" See, when you have debt, that means you have less money to work with in the market. I tell people it is imperative that they get out of debt before they try to put their money in the market because when your money is divided, you can't multiply it. Divided money doesn't make money. Multiplied money makes money.

Your financial freedom number needs this process of creating a business system to reach its destination. Remember that abundance is your destiny. Your goal is to become abundance attractive. You have to rid yourself of the poverty mentality. Currency flows to wherever it is welcomed. Decide that you will be a great steward over what's in your hand now, and as a result, more money will be added to you.

There is a story in the Bible that stands out to me. Each year I read it, I get a different revelation. Years ago, when I first read it, it was about how to be a great money manager. Today, it's about being a great money multiplier. You may know what the story is, and I'm going to summarize it here, as I've already told the story earlier in this book.

It's the story told in Matthew 25 in which a ruler gave three of his servants some money before he went away. When he came back, he wanted an account. He was like, "Hey, let's do some accounting here. I want to know what you did with the money I gave you." The first servant multiplied his money. The ruler was really happy. He gave this servant cities to rule over because he had come back to find a surplus, and he took that surplus and was able to multiply it. The same thing happened with the second servant. The third servant, however, had done nothing because of his fear of losing his master's money. He had hidden the money in the ground and then returned it to his master with no surplus, with no interest. The story goes on to say that the master was so angry that he actually threw this third servant out into the darkness where there were gnashing teeth heard (that sounds like Hell to me). He threw him there not because he didn't manage his money but because he didn't multiply his money. That's how important it is, even to God, that you move past the stage of just being a great money manager and become a great money multiplier.

That's what it's all about. We were created to multiply money, not just manage money. First, you have to learn to master it before you can begin to multiply it. That was the goal. Even for having spending plans, the goal is always to position yourself in a place where you are able to multiply your money. That's the revelation that I got out of it.

YOUR PERSONAL
CURRENCY MAP!

**How much money do you need to make each month
to live the life you REALLY want?**

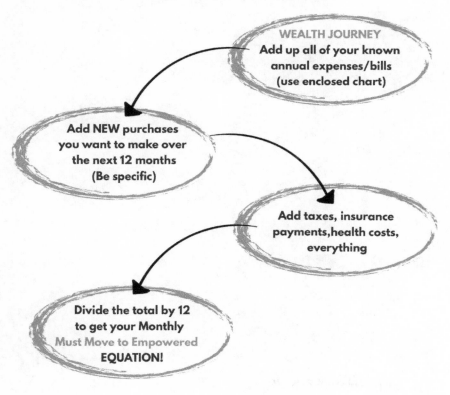

WEALTH JOURNEY
**Add up all of your known
annual expenses/bills
(use enclosed chart)**

**Add NEW purchases
you want to make over
the next 12 months
(Be specific)**

**Add taxes, insurance
payments, health costs,
everything**

**Divide the total by 12
to get your Monthly**
Must Move to Empowered
EQUATION!

DESTINATION WEALTH

EXPENSE	ANNUAL AMOUNT
Example: Mortgage / Rent	$20,000
TOTAL ANNUAL AMOUNT:	

TOTAL ANNUAL AMOUNT _____ Divided by 12 _____ = _____

MONTHLY FINANCIAL GOAL: $_____

FINANCIAL FREEDOM NUMBER

CHAPTER 11

Financial Bubbles and Cycles

We are living in a unique time in history. There is uncertainty everywhere. Where there is no certainty, people are fearful, and millions don't know how to use uncertain times to create wealth. The Bible says that the sons of Issachar knew how to discern the times and as a result of that understanding, they knew what their strategy should be. Their knowledge allowed them to have a PLAN FOR PROFIT. If you don't have a plan for wealth, you will not be obtaining it anytime soon. For the most part, the time value of money isn't on the procrastinator's side. Nor is it on the side of the financially ignorant. Remember, people with a low financial IQ rarely raise their heads high enough to see opportunity. Learning the cycles of money and about bubbles is a game-changer for anyone who wants to build wealth.

The United States government, as well as other major governments worldwide, are operating at unprecedented levels of debt. Interest rates are going to begin to rise in the US, after being zero or nearly zero for a decade after the 2008/2009 Great Recession. We are dealing with currency issues that affect foreign debt. We are also seeing more and more evidence of a global slowdown as economies like China and Germany are showing much less growth than we are accustomed to. The US dollar is the world's reserve currency (meaning that the US dollar is THE currency that is held in significant quantities by governments and institutions as part of their foreign exchange reserves), but even that tide is changing.

As I am typing this chapter, countries like Russia, China, and Turkey are hoping to start doing business in their own currencies, which means the days of world governments buying oil in US dollars are numbered. Each major power has gone through its time as the world's reserve, starting all the way back with Portugal when they were a reigning world power. That crown rotated around the world, stopping in France, and Great Britain, and most recently, after World War II, we became the world's reserve. But now, with our levels of debt, which are the highest they've ever been, we are going to be handing over that crown soon as well.

What I am trying to say is, the world is changing. Economies are changing. In fact, ever since the internet disrupted the communication of the world, economies change every three years now. The strategies that your grandparents used won't work in today's economy. That is because of things called cycles. The universal order from the greatest magnitudes of space, down to the atom, are all based on cycles. Subatomic particles cycle around each other like our planet cycles around the sun. What goes up, must come down. We rinse and repeat. However, depending on external circumstances, these cycles can be drastically exaggerated. The stock market, like everything else, also moves in cycles.

There are "bubbles" that form in one or multiple industries that inflate the upward movement of the economic cycle and make the deflating action of the cycle even more drastic. Most recently, there was the dot-com bubble in the late '90s and early 2000s, and then the real estate bubble in 2008. But cycles and bubbles date back farther than that—these are just the most recent ones.

As everyone reading this book can remember, a lot of people lost everything in the 2008 crash. People lost homes, jobs, and even their lives. It was something that seemed completely out of the blue and caught everyone by surprise. That is, everyone except the knowledgeable. Those who took the time to investigate saw the cheap plywood that propped up the real estate market. They saw through the smoke and mirrors while everyone else was more than happy to not play along and realize that time for what it was: too good to be true.

If you haven't seen the movie *The Big Short*, I would definitely recommend it. It tells the story of a few stock market investors who figured out the whole foundation of the real estate boom was built on fluff and corruption. They did the work, looked just a little deeper than others were willing to look, and they made out like fats cats. See, the thing is that money doesn't disappear. It's like energy. Energy cannot be created or destroyed; it is simply transferred. Now, money is created and obviously can be physically destroyed, but stay with me here. Whenever there is a huge economic crash and there are fortunes being lost, there are fortunes being made somewhere else. They are being made by people who leverage their knowledge of cycles. Going back to the idea of opportunity recognition, the people who recognize these opportunities are those who have taken the time to seek specialized education so that they can see the subtle tides moving that create these colossal waves. That is why we enrolled Adam in that stock investing class. We are not going to be caught with our pants down twice.

To be aware of these cycles, you have to seek knowledge. You have to take the time to look deeper than the average American. And you DEFINITELY can't ask your CFP because they are clueless. They are salespeople who are on the left side of the Cashflow Quadrant®.

You see, most people are like insects who live life skating across the surface of the water. They pay no attention to what is going on in the depths below. They only concern themselves with their microcosm of the world. Their job, their family, their personal problems. They take no time to observe problems on the macroeconomic scale, the problems, circumstances, and trends that impact us all, what is happening on a national and often international scale. Then, when a wave comes along, they are out of luck because they weren't like the fish living beneath the water.

See, the fish have a different perspective. They operate in a different world and position themselves in an environment where they see not only what is happening on the surface, but they also observe the currents underneath that influence it all. They notice the changing underlying currents and move to a more favorable position when they need to. Their new position then allows them to profit off those shifting currents. They use those currents to propel them further downstream, to push them closer toward their vision. When you are unprepared for wealth transfers due to cycles and bubbles, it's like the five foolish virgins in the bible. You miss out on OPPORTUNITIES.

Having a wealthy mindset is all about being in sync with your environment. It is about timing and taking advantage of dispensations in time. Important periods of time that represent major opportunity, like we talked about in the chapter on opportunity recognition. The wealthy are aware and in sync with the world around them. They sync their moves, their actions, their plans in accordance with the shifting tides of the world.

Until you are big enough to make your own waves, like Warren Buffet and his multi-billion-dollar market turning investment funds, you have to focus on catching the tailwinds of the waves made by national and international consumer trends, political climates, etc. We can use cycles to give us advanced notice of where we should be investing our money and participate in the trends in the market that make money—no matter what economy we are in, good or bad. You are making a great investment in yourself and your future just by reading this book, but you can't stop now. This book is about exposing you to opportunity and to what is available to you if you are willing to shift into the correct mindset, focus your ultimate goals and ambitions, and change your environment and habits in pursuit of this. But it is up to you to seek out advanced knowledge of these trends and cycles to truly take advantage of them.

The wealthy profit by piggybacking off of trends. If there is war, they invest in steel, rubber, aluminum, weapons, and oil. If there is a widespread illness, they invest in the treatment for it, or they might even invest in things that spread the illness, as horrible as that is, because it is profitable. For example, they might invest in the over-prescription of opioids and the subsidization of those that prescribed them.

You can choose what trends you want to take advantage of, but the bottom line is that there are a million different potentially profitable trends happening at any second. Choose one—heck, choose a couple—and really dive into those things, whether it's real estate, the stock market, a new product in line with consumer demand (like a drone with increased carrying capacity for larger food and general delivery orders). Acquire skills and knowledge that help you not only to make your own wealth but to preserve what you have.

In that same vein, I am not a fan of just handing your money off to a brokerage firm to invest blindly in the market. That's not investing because you don't learn anything by writing a check and mailing it every month. How much have you learned about cycles doing that? Your money shouldn't be treated like a cheap date. Most CFPs are salespeople, not investors. They are EMPLOYEES on the left side of the Cashflow Quadrant®.

Years ago, when Rob and I were just starting out on our journey of multiplying our money, we met with two financial planners. One was from American Express, and the other was from State Farm. I remember all too well the lady from American Express telling us that we couldn't afford to do real estate, yet she found money in the budget she created for us to pay her $400 a month to invest in a mutual fund. I felt uneasy. Not because I was uneducated about mutual funds but because I knew she didn't have our best interests in mind. She didn't listen to what was important to us. She told us to take our kids out of private school and to use the money to invest with her instead. Then, as if this wasn't enough, I guess I wasn't moving fast enough for her in signing the agreement, and so she called me and said, "You are taking too long and are going to make me miss my bonus."

BINGO – there you have it. Out of the abundance of the heart, the mouth speaks. We were her meal ticket. She needed us to make her quota for the month. Needless to say, I told her to stick her binder where the sun don't shine, and we invested in real estate like we had planned. As I've mentioned a few times, we made $47,000 from our first real estate deal. We then made $500,000 from our second real estate deal. Now, no mutual fund would have done that for me in two years. This is why knowing about cycles and bubbles is so important. The old, conventional teachings of buy, hold, and diversify just don't work in this economy. The new way to build wealth is to keep your money working in tandem with the current cycles and bubbles.

What I learned from this experience is that you don't learn how to invest by just writing someone a check. Most CFPs are not educated in cycles, bubbles, and investing strategies. Furthermore, they don't spend time looking back to follow trends. I would recommend you read the book *The Little Book of Stock Market Cycles* by Jeffrey A. Hirsch, but in the meantime, I will give you a crash course. Knowing about stock market cycles and utilizing this knowledge to make investment decisions is a wonderful strategy for multiplying your money. Winston Churchill once said, "The farther back you can look, the farther forward you are likely to see."

Investment Cycle Education

Q. What are cycles?

A. Cycles are **repeating patterns** that occur in nature. Our circadian rhythms, heartbeats, tides, weather patterns, and seasons are all cycles. Cycles also occur in financial markets. Our world contains over almost 5,000 cycles **"for which there is no logical explanation and no known cause. The important thing about regularity is that it implies predictability. And if you know an event is coming, you can often prevent it or avoid it if you wish. Or if you cannot prevent or avoid it, you can at least prepare for it so that its effect on your life is lessened."** - Edward Dewey.

In the world of investing, a cycle is an amalgamation of the most effective indicators and patterns and that have been researched and tracked. Those who study cycles and learn to leverage them are likely to profit from their efforts. Now, stock market cycles are not always exact, but they are worth following.

Q. What is a "bubble"?

A. A bubble, also referred to as an economic bubble, asset bubble, speculative bubble, price bubble, or market bubble, is when an asset is trading at a price range that far exceeds its actual intrinsic value. In other words, the value of the asset has been inflated and essentially isn't worth what the market is currently valuing it for. Bubbles are fueled by exuberant market behavior and are created by a sudden increase in asset price that is not justified or necessary when you look at the fundamentals of the asset. Bubbles are characterized by the speedy escalation of asset prices, followed by a contraction. A bubble deflates when no more investors are willing to buy at the inflated price, and a massive sell-off occurs. That is when the bubble "pops."

The 5 Steps of a Bubble, as told by Investopedia:

1. Displacement: This phase begins when investors notice some sort of event or shift in the paradigm, such as a new product, extremely

low interest rates, ground-breaking technology, or something else that grabs their attention and screams "opportunity."

2. Boom: As the first investors get in, prices begin to rise. They continue to gain momentum as more investors become aware of the opportunity and jump on the bandwagon. The foundation for the boom is being set. FOMO (fear of missing out) begins to take hold.

3. Euphoria: Asset prices skyrocket as everyone and their mother want in on what seems to them like the opportunity of a lifetime. This paradigm-shifting technology or market trend has now become mainstream knowledge, and all caution is forgotten.

4. Profit (for some): Once a bubble pops, it will not inflate again. Not anytime soon, at least. It is very difficult to gauge when a bubble will pop, but it is better to be safe, and check out with the profits you have, than to be caught on the wrong side of it. Those who look at the warning signs will see the small indications of ensuing collapse, sell off their positions, and most likely profit handsomely.

5. Panic: The buyers are exhausted, as the market realizes that the asset class or technology in question is extremely overvalued, with prices well exceeding its true worth. Massive sell-offs occur, and prices drop as quickly as they rose. Investors move to liquidate their assets at any price, as supply overwhelmingly outgrows demand.

Q. How do cycles work?

A. **Patterns repeat over certain periods of time.** There are cycles for each thing; not everything is on the same cycle. Sometimes, cycles converge at the same time and create more drastic variation—for example, a very cold winter or a drastic downturn in the market.

Q. Why doesn't everyone know about cycles?

A. Cycles in the stock market were first discovered in the 1930s, right after the Great Depression, and the elite weren't interested in sharing the information learned with the less fortunate in society. Only top educators, like MIT, the Smithsonian, and the Carnegie Institute were invited to learn about them, along with a handful of powerful politicians and wealthy entrepreneurs. They used the information for their own gain and did not share it with the population at large. They are still used by sovereign governments, financial institutions (like Goldman Sachs), billionaires, and learned traders/investors, but not the average person or financial advisor.

Q. How does this apply to me?

A. By using cycles, **you can see patterns and indicators** arising that can be predictive of big turns in markets, when certain investments are bottoming, etc. If you are prepared for these events in advance, you can position yourself to take advantage of them when the time comes. **Imagine if you had advanced warning for the peak of the tech bubble or the housing crisis of 2008. How much would that have helped your financial situation?** The answer to that question actually hinges on how much you know. There are two major knowledge components necessary to take advantage of cycles. First, you have to be educated on the indicators so you can know what trends to look for that signify a bubble has formed—and secondly, you need to know the length of time of the asset bubble.

Q. Is following cycles the same as market timing?

A. No, market timers try to "trade" the market with frequent buy-and-sell signals.

Q. Do these cycles really work?

A. Yes, but don't just take it from me. Here is another quote:

"But, working quietly behind the scenes, **thousands of scientists** in fields as unrelated as history, botany, anthropology, mammalogy, terrestrial magnetism, sociology, and economics—to name only a few—are accumulating facts and figures that promise to make this age-old dream of **foretelling the future** at least a partial reality. **A new science** which deals with the behavior of events **recurring at reasonably regular intervals throughout the universe** may ultimately enable us **to predict, scientifically and accurately, the events of tomorrow.**"

While no one has a crystal ball, cycles are a very helpful indicator of what is likely to happen.

Q. How hard is it to use information about cycles to invest?

A. Knowing where to invest in the next bubble can be **tremendously lucrative**, especially if you are early into the investment. Knowing when to get out before a change in trend is also very valuable. Riding the right wave and avoiding the wrong one, I believe, will prove to make a great difference to your investing and ultimately, wealth.

Every investment class (e.g., stocks, commodities, real estate, cryptocurrencies, bonds, and cash equivalents) has a cycle and the occasional bubble.

- Real Estate, on average, has an 18-year cycle
  - This fact was observed by renowned real estate market researcher Homer Hoyt in 1933.
  - Economist Brad Case of Nareit outlines, in his article "Looking Carefully at the Current Real Estate Market Cycle," the cycles that the real estate market has completed in my lifetime. Since I have been alive, we have completed two cycles and are in a third.
    - September 1972-August 1989
      - Duration: 16 years, 11 months
      - Duration of Downturn: 27 months
      - Duration of Recovery: 21 months
      - Duration of Expansion: 155 months
    - August 1989-January 2007
      - Duration: 17 years, 5 months
      - Duration of Downturn: 14 months
      - Duration of Recovery: 5 months
      - Duration of Expansion: 190 months
    - January 2007-Present
      - Duration: 12 years and counting
      - Duration of Downturn: 25 months
      - Duration of Recovery: **41 months** (called the Great Recession for a reason)
      - Duration of Expansion: 77 months to date
- Stocks have a 4-5-year cycle
  - Stocks have both short-term and long-term cycles

- Terminology check: "Bull market" means the market is going up, whereas "bear market" means that the market is going down. If a stock is "bullish," it is going up. If a stock is "bearish," it is going down.
- Short-term cycles are called "cyclical cycles" and typically last 4 years, with bear and bull phases lasting 1-3 years each.
- Long-term cycles are called "secular cycles" and tend to last around 30 years, with bear and bull market phases lasting 10-20 years each. A secular cycle is one that is driven by forces that were in place and which act for many years on the price of a particular investment or asset class. This influence would cause that security or asset class to rise or fall over a long period of time.
- It is possible to exist in a cyclical bull phase, and a secular bear phase, and vice versa, at the same time. Take early 2011 for example. The US stock market was in a cyclical bull phase and had been in an uptrend for multiple years. However, most experts agreed that the US stock market was still in a secular bear phase since it had been stagnant since the market peaked in 2000.
- Commodities typically have a 15-year cycle.
  - However, they also have "super cycles" that can last from 10-35 years.
  - Tradable commodities include
    - metals (e.g., gold, silver, copper)
    - energy (e.g., natural gas, crude oil)
    - livestock/meat (e.g., live cattle, hogs, pork belly)
    - agricultural (e.g., soybeans, sugar, corn)
  - Whenever stock markets turn bearish (downward) or inflation increases, many people transfer their money to gold, which is a reliable store of value.
  - An example of a commodities cycle can be found in the early 2000s commodities boom (2000-2014).
    - This cycle began following the Great Commodities Depression of the 1980s and 1990s.

- It was created in lieu of the 2007-2008 housing bubble, as people shifted their money over to commodities, which were seen as a much safer bet.
- The whole theory is that since commodities are traded for actual usage, and their prices are based firmly on supply and demand. On the flip side, stock prices are heavily susceptible to speculation, news, and sentiment.
- Despite money shifting from the housing crisis, the commodities boom was mostly the result of increased demand from emerging global markets such as Brazil, Russia, India, and especially China.
- Each commodity has a different story to tell, but generally, from 2000-2014, everything from gold, to oil, to chlorine, experienced a subsequent period of rapid inflation and eventual return.

- Bonds have a 30-35-year cycle.
  - Governments, corporations, and municipalities issue bonds when they need capital.
  - Bonds have been around for millennia.
  - Bonds tend to be conservative investments that are generally considered a safer alternative to the rigorous stock market.
  - Most bonds pay a fixed income that won't change. Bond prices depend on the value investors place on the income the bond provides. Bonds accrue interest—the longer-term the bond, the higher the interest paid.
  - The most recent bond cycle lasted from 1981-2011.
- Cryptocurrencies are a new asset class. They, too, have a life cycle, but they haven't been around long enough to for a verifiable pattern to be established. This is especially true as they are still looking to find a bottom to settle at as of the end of 2018.

No one in the world cares more about your finances than you should. If that isn't true for you, then you don't deserve to be wealthy in the first place. But for the majority of people for whom that statement rings true, why is it so far-fetched when people suggest you learn how to master your own money? I get people who come up to me all the time saying they want to learn how to invest. What should I be investing in? Can you tell me what to invest in? And I can honestly say that an investment in your knowledge, an investment in your education, should not only be your first step but that it literally pays the biggest dividends.

Having a knowledge of cycles is very important also because they help you distinguish real and profitable opportunities from all the riff-raff you hear about in Facebook comments or from your shifty uncle with a limp who sits in the barbershop giving financial investment advice.

Take cryptocurrency in 2018 for example. Last year, Bitcoin took the news by storm, and cryptocurrencies became the hottest thing since sliced bread. Celebrities, from DJ Khaled to Floyd Mayweather, were creating their own cryptocurrencies or promoting investment in crypto offerings. Everyone wanted a piece of the action because anything having to do with cryptocurrency was seen as the new golden investment opportunity. Never mind that a few people knew or cared how crypto or its underlying (and much more valuable) technology, blockchain, worked.

Whenever you get wind of a new opportunity, you have to research and gather a good understanding (or at least an educated guess) as to which stage of the cycle a trend or opportunity is currently in. In the realm of crypto, the time to get into Bitcoin would have been between 2009-2010. My husband and I first found out about Bitcoin in 2009. So, in 2019, when your barber, the UPS guy, and grocery checkout person are all talking about how they're saving up to buy their first hundredth of a bitcoin, why is it that people think that this is the time to get in on it? If people would stop long enough to consider many of the opportunities they invest in from an objective standpoint, they would save themselves so much capital and headache.

The Bitcoin bubble burst in 2018. Peaking at an all-time high of $19,511 in December of 2017, the world-renowned cryptocurrency and talk of the town began an epic plunge into 2018 that would see a loss of around 82% of that value. POP. Now, this does not mean that Bitcoin is dead. It has recovered from a number of bubbles, including a 2011 crash that was almost as devastating as the most recent one.

Even given the crashes, early Bitcoin investors who have held their coins since Bitcoin first came onto the scene in 2009 or got in in those first couple of years still came out in the positive even after the latest bubble. Even though it is down substantially from its peak, the Bitcoin price is still triple what it was at the beginning of 2017.

Those who sold off at or near the peak made out like fat cats. They recognized an opportunity. They got in on the bubble early. They acknowledged that there was a cycle at work, as there always is, and they got out when it started to seem too good to be true. Self-control is an important underlying factor in all this. You have to have self-control and discipline to resist the urge to get in when everyone else is getting in, the opportunity has become mainstream, and you have missed most of the value that it had to offer. It also takes self-control to get out when you are enjoying the advantages of an opportunity that just seems to get better and better.

Nothing gold can stay. It's a quote from a famed book called *The Outsiders*, and it always rings true. You have to be aware of what's called "irrational exuberance," a term pegged by former Federal Reserve Chairman Alan Greenspan. It refers to a situation when a stock is overvalued and has extreme popularization When your barber, the delivery man, the preacher, and everyone else is talking about an investment opportunity, that's irrational exuberance. When you are at a dinner party or the salon, and everyone is talking about a particular investment, run in the opposite direction. When you are in an investment that is simply going through the roof, you have to be realistic with yourself when you start to feel something breathing down your neck. You have to listen to that little voice in the back of your head that tells you, even in the middle of all the fun you're having, that your fun can't last forever. It's like the thought you have on the flight to a vacation destination—that one stray sorrowful thought of how sad the plane ride back will be, which interrupts the excited thoughts you're having. How much it will suck that all the fun is over. Self-control gives credence to this voice. It acknowledges it because it is the truth, not simply something that is trying to bring you down.

So, when you're in something that seems like it can soar forever, realize that it simply cannot. Everything goes in cycles, ups and downs, booms and crashes. It is those that won't acknowledge that who are left hanging out to dry. One such person in the case of Bitcoin was John McAfee, the extremely wealthy founder of the cybersecurity company McAfee LLC (we all know the little boxes that pop up and say it's time to renew your McAfee cybersecurity plan and you exit out because it's blocking the 1-day shipping tab on Amazon). On December 7th, he tweeted: "Bitcoin now at $16,600. Those of you in the old school who believe this is a bubble simply have not understood the new mathematics of the Blockchain, or you did not care enough to try. Bubbles are mathematically impossible in this new paradigm. So are corrections and all else." This was a few days before the price briefly peaked at its all-time high and then proceeded to start its epic plunge that can safely be classified as a bubble bursting. No investment is impervious to cycles. Every opportunity has an expiration. Recognize it, seize it, and then know when to let go.

It is also important to be able to discern what opportunity lies within the cycle you are investigating. While cryptocurrency is going through a tough time, it is the currency of the future. Everything will eventually be digital. I do not deny that. Whether the cryptocurrency that ends up being the world's go-to currency is Bitcoin, however, is yet to be determined. There are those that must fall on the sword so that eventually someone can break the precedent and make history.

Many people thought Hillary Clinton would be the first female president. Maybe she should have been. Regardless of your feelings on the outcome of the election, she still played an important role, even though she didn't achieve what she set out to do. Maybe Bitcoin is not the last and final crypto-giant. But whatever takes its place would not be there if Bitcoin hadn't gone through the market and regulatory journeys it is undergoing now.

But back to discerning the real value of an opportunity going through a cycle. Blockchain, the technology that Bitcoin and other cryptocurrencies are based on, has limitless potential in almost every sector. It can be, and currently is, being implemented into every industry, from grocery, to agriculture, to automotive, to traditional banking. Blockchain is extremely valuable and will be around for a long time, regardless of whether crypto is. So, you have to be able to recognize the lifespan and cycles of opportunities within opportunities. Find the diamond in the rough. Find the piece of that opportunity that has a cycle with much more longevity than the opportunity on the surface.

When the real estate bubble expanded, many people viewed it as their opportunity to buy properties and houses at rates that were never thought to be possible. People flipped houses, purchased their dream homes, and saw the gradually inflating bubble as an opportunity, not realizing that it was a bubble that was readily nearing a burst. Conversely, educated people decided to do their research and look a little deeper, and they realized that we were building a multimillion-dollar mansion on a glass foundation. A drive-thru worker with bad credit was getting approved for loans of whatever amount they wanted. They were selling homes to whoever. Then, that faulty debt was getting packaged up with less crappy debt and sold off as not as bad of a ticking time bomb as it truly was.

Those who saw this took advantage of the opportunity, of course. They shorted the market and made out like fat cats. But people like Warren Buffet, Bill Gates and Robert Kiyosaki, and other learned real estate investors also leveraged their knowledge of cycles and bubbles. They realized that these over-inflated property prices were not going to last. I don't want to butcher the story, but in one of his books, Robert Kiyosaki speaks about how he and some of his real estate associates were presented with the opportunity to buy a huge resort in Arizona. The resort was comprised of five golf courses and was originally for sale during the real estate bubble for an insane amount. I cannot recall the exact amount, but it was insane. Somewhere upward of $70 million. Kiyosaki saw that the value was overinflated, and instead waited on the opportunity until the opportunity's cycle aligned with his interests. After the bubble burst, the resort went into foreclosure, where Kiyosaki acquired it for $46 million in bankruptcy court. He not only purchased it for significantly less than the original price, but Kiyosaki had purchased the property for around 25% of what the previous owner had invested into the property. His knowledge of bubbles and cycles literally saved him tens of millions of dollars. That is the power of APPLIED knowledge.

While I am on the topic of real estate, I might as well cover one of the biggest and most painful bubbles in history: the aforementioned real estate bubble of 2008. I am about to give you a bit of financial education history, but bear with me here, and hopefully, I can help you realize that there is a much bigger picture behind what happened in 2007-2008, despite many of us only focusing on a corner piece of that picture.

It actually all began way back in 1971 when President Nixon took us off the gold standard. See, the dollar was only worth something because it was backed by gold. This means that every US dollar represented a certain amount of gold—gold which existed, which was worth something, and which was sitting safely in a bank vault somewhere. When Nixon took us off the gold standard, he essentially said that the dollar no longer had to be backed by a certain amount of gold, effectively lifting the restrictions on him being able to print a bunch of money.

That is exactly what he did. Money was now considered fiat money, and thus, it had ZERO value. The United States' printing presses were turned on (also called quantitative easing) as Nixon's government printed these "counterfeit" dollars in order to fund its debts and expenses. These dollars were poured into Saudi Arabia, because the US used a lot of oil, and that occurred just as oil prices began to rise.

With the rising cost of oil, more and more of these "petrodollars," as they came to be called, needed to find a home. These Arab countries had to store that money somewhere. So, they put them in banks in London. London banks were large enough to handle such a sudden increase in cash. The money could not simply sit in London banks, however, and so they loaned it out, of course. They loaned the petrodollars to anyone who would borrow them, which Latin American countries gladly did.

As a result of this sudden influx of cash which was not a result of increased economic output, the Latin American economy went into a bubble phase from the late 1970s to the early 1980s and then burst. This is known today as the Latin American debt crisis.

Those petrodollars then moved from a ruined Latin America to Japan. In Japan, they then experienced a bubble that inflated and popped in 1989. That money then hot-potatoed its way through Mexico, where it induced the Mexican peso crisis of 1994. It then moved on to Asia where it plunged them into crisis in 1997. Not long after, the petrodollars landed in Russia and casued the Russian ruble crisis of 1998.

The US managed to balance its budget while Clinton was in office from 1993-2001. That meant that the US government was not looking to borrow any money, which was bad news for bankers around the world who were desperately looking for more borrowers to borrow in the trillions. Well, they found luck with Fannie Mae and Freddie Mac. Now, you may have heard these names before, but aren't exactly familiar with what these companies are or what they do. They are GSEs (government sponsored enterprises) that play a pivotal role in the mortgage industry. Fannie and Freddie buy mortgages from lenders, pool them together, and then sell them to investors as mortgaged backed securities. Together, they borrowed between $3 to $5 trillion of this hot-potato money and loaned it to pretty much everyone who wanted to refinance their home or buy a new one. This is how the real estate bubble that spawned the Great Recession was blown.

Once Freddie Mac and Fannie May came under investigation, they stopped borrowing this money, but by then, the damage had been done. These petrodollars needed to find a new home, and in the late '90s, government officials, like President Clinton and then-Federal Chair Alan Greenspan changed the rules for the country's biggest banks, including the Bank of America, Goldman Sachs, and Citigroup. These banks began taking in this money after those rules were changed. Cash has to keep flowing, that is why it is called currency.

Mortgage brokers working for companies like Countrywide Mortgage started looking for anyone who wanted to borrow money in order to help the banks and Wall Street move this tainted money. They dove into the poorest of the poor neighborhoods across the country and offered "NINJA" loans to millions of people who were unemployed and had no credit. Now, some of you might have heard of these before, but for those who haven't, NINJA stands for "no income, no job or asset". Essentially, these people did not have to have any means to be able to pay these loans back. Families across the nation got to make their American Dream a reality. But they did not know the true nightmare that was the housing bubble, which was quickly inflating into a hot air balloon.

To add insult to injury, Wall Street and the banks packaged this toxic debt and sold it as assets after these subprime mortgages were processed. They basically sandwiched together toxic debt with not-so-toxic debt in order to make it look better. They spray-painted the turd golden. These new debt sandwiches with mixed good and bad debt in were called MBSs (mortgage backed securities) and CDOs (collateralized debt obligations). They were the derivatives of subprime debt packaged as prime. (For anyone who is lost, toxic debt is simply debt that someone owes that you know they will not be able to pay back.)

Well, essentially they started trading this debt on the market. So now the potential for financial disaster just got so much bigger, because not only are the banks and families involved going to be affected when the bubble bursts, but every entity and anyone associated with it who was playing hot potato with these ticking debt time bombs was also affected. The biggest banks and Wall Street sold these stinky debt sandwiches as ASSETS (the nerve) to other banks, pension funds, and investors INTERNATIONALLY. It was like they were bottling air and selling it as a weight loss pill.

Even the ratings agencies were in on it, as Warren Buffett's rating company, Moody's, was giving AAA ratings to these toxic-debt-bundled CDOs like they didn't know they were toxic. They sold this debt all over the world, and global home prices soared. Many all over the world felt they had accomplished the American Dream as the deceiving "wealth effect" swept across housing markets internationally. The wealth effect I speak of is a situation that makes a person feel wealthier than they actually are because their home increases in value. In reality, that is just capital gains. That is not something that is continuously putting money in your pocket. It's transitory. People confused an increase in home value with an increase in net worth, and that simply isn't the case. But this misplaced enthusiasm and increased but skewed perception of increased wealth caused people to swipe credit cards like there was no tomorrow. Then, they would pay off their credit cards by refinancing their homes, further blowing up the bubble!

I am not sure how many of you are familiar with the movie *The Big Short*, but it's a great movie which I have already mentioned but want to recommend again here. It's about a few traders who took the time to investigate what was going on in 2007-2008. They uncovered the glass foundation that the house of faux prosperity was built on. They leveraged that information into a fortune once the bubble finally burst.

The most demoralizing part was how disgusted they were that the smartest people in America had sat back and let this happen. All the people who we praise as being fiscal and monetary policy geniuses, banking geniuses, and stock market geniuses were all in on the biggest scam of our lifetime. Fannie Mae and Freddie Mac knew the government would bail them out. It cost $150 billion to do it, but they knew the government would do it. The banks and brokers knew they were selling off toxic debt and didn't care. The real estate brokers selling these mansions to auto mechanics knew there was no way they should be selling them that house. The banks knew that these people didn't qualify for these loans, and yet they granted them anyways.

One of the characters in *The Big Short*, played by Steve Carrell, was so disillusioned that he stopped working in the stock industry altogether, took his fortune, and moved to a nice quiet little area where he didn't have to be confronted with the dark reality that is the true face of our banking system.

So, I have taken you back to the deepest-rooted cause of the housing crash of 2007-2008. With roots that date back decades, and money that circulated all over the world. Yet, the majority of people had no idea that this ticking petrodollar timebomb was making its global rounds destroying one economy after the next.

I wanted to give you a real-life example of how this happened and how we lived through it, yet some people are still none the wiser. They just think it was a random unfortunate event. Nothing is random, and if you think it is, you just aren't looking deep enough. The ignorant man will see things as random; the knowledgeable man will expect what the ignorant man doesn't. The Bible says that by wisdom a house is built, but knowledge fills its rooms.

This is why I always say that an informed, educated consumer is the best consumer. I want you to be able to expect the things that catch others off guard. Fortunes are made when opportunity disguised as tragedy arrives. It's been this way since the beginning of time. Those who aren't prepared will have their wealth transferred into the hands of the prepared. So, stay conscious of global events. Look for the shifting tides and understand that if everything moves in cycles, you can time your moves to your benefit. You can be that "lucky" rich guy on the right side of history because it is not actually about luck; it's about being prepared. It's important that you understand that the world is indifferent to you. People up and down the housing, real estate, and banking food chains knew people would lose their cars, homes, and in a lot of cases, their lives if they were dragged into this mess. But everyone was trying to get their piece. So, you can't feel bad about getting yours. The Bible says the wealth of the wicked is set up for the righteous. Claim your knowledge so that you can claim your wealth.

Another reason I can speak to this subject so well is that my husband and I got caught up in the irrational exuberance of the real estate craze. We also lost money on beautiful waterfront properties in North Carolina. We got in when the bubble was almost at its peak. Although I wasn't one of those who bought a home they couldn't afford (I actually paid cash for my land and built my own primary residence), I was buying overpriced real estate as an investment. So, after that expensive lesson, I decided that I would never be in that position again, and I started to educate myself on cycles and bubbles.

You must be able to identify market indicators so that you can devise the right investment strategy. Indicators will help reveal at what point in the cycle you are in. It will help you answer a lot of the most basic questions: If interest rates go up, what should I be doing? What should I be doing with interest rates drop? What should I be doing if inflation becomes high? How do I know if the country is experiencing deflation? What about stagflation? All of these involve financial education terms or phenomena that I could write a whole other book on, but right now, I simply want to bring them to your attention and challenge you to go about the process of self-education. You have the world at your fingertips. All it takes is a few Google searches, and, of course, considering multiple sources, to have a solid idea of what the implications of rising interest rates or inflation are. When interest rates fall, that's a good time to be looking at real estate, invest in cash-rich companies, or refinance your existing loans to get lower interest rates. When interest rates go up, bonds become attractive. You get the picture. All of these indicators come with strategies to increase your money.

Once you become knowledgeable in the various cycles that affect money on a national, as well as local, scale, you can begin to rotate your attention through those cycles depending on which is the best time to get in. Cycles are like buses. They more or less follow the same route. Now, there are always "black swan" events (e.g., war, famine, natural disasters, etc.) that can impact and throw off the timing of these cycles. But excluding those outlying events, cycles repeat themselves on a pretty predictable basis. Each bus has a different route. Each sector has a different cycle. There are many routes you could take on the road to financial freedom to your dream lifestyle. Through your knowledge of cycles, however, you can get on and off certain buses at the exact right times to get to your destination as soon as possible. Now, no one is perfect, and you will get greedy and stay in a trade too long. You will mistime an entry or an exit. There will be outlying events that disrupt the cycles' timing. However, even with those inevitable setbacks, your knowledge of cycles will allow you to effectively invest both your time and money.

If you are in real estate making good money, and you see it is coming up on the end of its 18-year cycle, it is time for you to exit if you are flipping properties. Maybe you then take the money you made from real estate and put it into the stock market. The stock market has a 4-5 year cycle. You seem to be right in the middle of it, and it is a good time to enter. With it being a good time in the stock market and a bad time in the real estate market, you can take the money you have invested in the real estate market and bet against the real estate market in the stock market. You look up real estate ETFs, place puts against the stock, or short the stock, and then you continue to make that real estate money work for you.

The alternative is to leave your money in the real estate market, naively think that it will continue to grow forever, and then lose everything you made much faster than it took you to make it once the bubble bursts. Say there is a breakdown in global trade that negatively impacts the stock market to the point where your investment is no longer viable, but you are at an advantageous phase in the bond market cycle, so you take your money out of stocks and put it in bonds. It is all about awareness in the jungle that is finance and investment. The more aware you are of your surroundings, the longer you survive and thrive.

The investor really doesn't always have their own perspective. So, that's one of the things that I'm trying to allow you to have: your own unique perspective, rather than allowing the media to feed you their perspective (by the way, these people are broadcasters, not investors), or magazine or periodicals, or a program showing you their perspective. It's really about you being able to look at the different market indicators yourself and determine what you should do. This way, you can have a personalized perspective such that, as you see things play out, you have a better understanding of the economy and will be able to identify where we are and where we are headed. I see that a lot of this stuff on television is just noise, and you have to learn how to separate the noise from what's really going on.

Markets move based on fear and greed. The fickle masses and mob psychology play a huge role in market cycles, specifically regarding how big these bubbles can get. In order for us to have a low, a bottom, in the stock market, we have to reach a maximum level of pessimism. In order to have a peak in the bubble, we have to reach a maximum level of optimism. Both can be exaggerated or misplaced, but they are powerful drivers, nonetheless. That is why markets can shoot up or down because of a sketchy news story or one of Donald Trump's tweets, or when Elon Musk tweeted that he was taking Tesla private. It didn't matter that he had no resources or a structure in place to make that happen. All that mattered were people's feelings when he said it. **We live in a world driven by sentiment, not facts.** That is why someone like Donald Trump can be elected even though a lot of his points are based on lies. Humans are emotional decision-makers; the best sellers tap into emotion.

I'd like to tell you a story that I read some years ago. It's a story about irrational exuberance. Joseph Kennedy, President John F. Kennedy's father, once went to the shoeshine boy to have his shoes shined. The shoeshine boy gave him a stock tip in September of 1929, telling him that he should really get into the market and that it was the perfect time. Joseph Kennedy went and sold all of his stock that day, because he said that if the shoeshine boy is in the market saying the same thing everyone else is, then there's nobody else who could come into the market and make it go up anymore.

The market turns around off its peak and dips when there are no buyers left. That happens when everyone and their mother is already in on it. That is maximum optimism. That's when the market is going to turn down. And so, of course, like I said, Joseph Kennedy sold his stock when he knew the shoeshine boy was interested. He saved himself from the crash of 1929. The crash transferred millions of dollars from the uninformed to the pockets of the well-informed. In 1929, mostly everybody lost everything they had, including the clothes off their backs. One of the key indicators of when a bubble is getting ready to burst and the market is getting ready to shift is when you hear everyone talking about an opportunity. We all experienced that with Bitcoin most recently, and we all experienced it in

2007 when everyone you knew was getting a new house and becoming a real estate broker.

I remember I had a friend who was telling me that his barber was telling him to invest in Iraqi dinar, which was ludicrous because there was no market for it, not even over in Iraq. But most people are ready and willing to take the advice of others that seem even marginally knowledgeable because they don't want to take the time to do the research themselves. Remember, if being wealthy was easy, everyone would be wealthy. If being financially free was easy, everyone would be financially free. How is it that people think that becoming wealthy is easy? Like all the work it takes on your part is a 20-minute conversation with someone who isn't even wealthy! Would you let your cousin Pooky do surgery on you if he said that everyone was doing it and it has worked out spectacularly for them? No! You would go to a doctor, someone with specialized training and years of experience. Why? Because that is common sense.

So, why is it that we do not have the same mentality with our money as we do with our health? It's because we want to believe it's that easy, even when, deep down, we know it's not. Stop fooling yourself and ending up on the deflated side of the bubble. All you are doing is making a more knowledgeable person wealthier by handing over your hard-earned (but poorly invested) money. True wealth whispers; it's not broadcast to the entire world. Billionaires move in silence.

Years ago, my investor, Dexter, called me and said, "LaShawne, they're opening up a new oil pipeline. Its an investment opportunity in Alaska with ExxonMobil. You can get in on the ground level and invest in it. I think this will be great for you and Robert to do at this time." I didn't know anything about investing in gas or oil, and I was petrified—or, you might say I was *petrol*fied. I was too scared to do it. Literally whenever I think about it now, I just want to kick myself over and over and over again for not doing it. Instead of listening to my investor, I listened to some people at my church, and Rob and I invested in something stupid that everybody was talking about; it was like throwing my money out of the window because I haven't seen a dime from that investment sense. I decided then that I would never take financial advice from a broke person, an uninformed person, or someone who doesn't have a proven track record with investing. That started my investment education, and now, I can tell people what to do because I've made enough mistakes so that you don't have to. I have learned, and now I love making my money multiply in the market.

I was afraid to invest with Exxon 20 years ago because I was ignorant about investing. I didn't know anything about it. Most life on Earth is similar in that everything fears what it does not know. Humans especially. I lacked sound investment education. If I had taken the time to do my own research and had invested in my investment education, I would've seen all the signs that pointed to the sound and profitable investment, not the one that sounded good but had no substance. I would have known that we were in a commodities market cycle back in 1996, and I could have made a boatload of money. That was a learning experience for me. I don't think I don't look at it as being a failure. I just look at it as being a learning experience. Like the saying goes, you either win or you learn.

So, I hope this chapter has helped shed some light on the fact that the world is much less "random" than we think. Cycles repeat. Asset classes go up and down in value. Bubbles form, economies rise and fall, and it all repeats sooner or later. If you know this, you can position yourself to profit, or at the very least avoid a position of immense loss.

CONCLUSION

I am glad to be able to scratch the surface and show you what is possible. This book is meant to whet your appetite. I wanted to gradually pull the curtain back for you because I find that tearing it back leaves people overwhelmed and fired up with no clear direction to go in.

There is a farming practice called tilling. It is when you stir or agitate soil to break up crusted soil so that the seeds you plant can take root. If you don't till the ground by shoveling and stirring the soil, the seeds will simply sit on the surface, wither, and die. We have covered a lot of things in this book. I began by tilling the ground. I needed to get you in a headspace to receive. I have come to learn that you can throw all the knowledge in the world at a person, but if they are not in the correct mindset, with the correct exposure and perspective, that knowledge will fall on deaf ears.

We began by talking about the different types of fear and addressing what has been holding you back. I want you to really be honest with yourself, identify that fear, and then conquer it through the means and exercises we covered throughout this book.

We then went Seven Layers Deep to help you discover your truest "WHY." We analyzed the core reasons why you are reading this book, why you want to fulfill your potential, why you want to be financially free, why you want to be wealthy, and why you get up in the morning and go to sleep late at night.

After you discover this, remember to write it down and keep it with you. It should be printed out and stuck on the ceiling above your bed, as far as I'm concerned, so that it's there as a reminder whenever you are nervous about sending that email, whenever you have doubts before that big meeting, whenever it seems like everything is crashing down around you and your dream doesn't seem within reach or worth it anymore.

You have to lean on your truest "WHY" because any cute or superficial "WHY" will not provide you with the kick in the butt and strength that you need.

We went from your truest "WHY" to your mindset, exposure, and the stages of learning. To be honest, I could write a whole book on mindset. To a certain extent, this book is completely about mindset. Every topic I have covered can be traced back to mindset, as it is the most important ASSET of the wealthy. No, I did not misspeak—your mindset is an asset. The correct mindset allows you to set the correct goals, recognize opportunities, see the value in investing in yourself, and realize that focusing on your strengths and leveraging your God-given talents allows you to provide the most good to the most people.

We also talked about the stages of learning. The stages which you actively experienced here are the stages that I want now you to experience in your life. I talked to you about exposure, and how, although you may have grown up with narrow horizons, it is now your responsibility to expand them. Get out there and see what is possible.

There are so many ways to make money, some of which you might never have envisioned yourself doing. Now, I am talking about legal stuff here, so keep everything above board, and don't do anything you couldn't tell your mother about. I never saw myself owning and servicing vending machines. However, without that intermediate step, I would not have been able to get into real estate. Stop thinking that what you have to do has to be ground-breaking from the start. Life is bound to bring you detours, but as long as you keep your ultimate goals in mind, like the founders of Airbnb did, you will ultimately arrive at your destination. Let me rephrase that: Your knowledge and willingness to see opportunity where others don't see it might bring you detours. But they aren't actually detours if they bring you closer to your ultimate goals. Open your mind and explore your options so that you can expand your means. Don't simply save and wait decades to get the money you need to take the next step.

We defined what true wealth is: time. True wealth is the freedom to spend your time how you wish after you have established wealth systems and assets that continue to make you money without your direct, hands-on involvement.

I introduced you to the phenomenon of epigenetics and the idea that your current mindset and wealth blueprint were inherited. But, just like they were changed by traumatic incidents all those years ago due to environmental stresses, they can also be changed for the better today. We are no longer slaves, so we should no longer think and behave like them. We should no longer have a scarcity mindset and poverty practices because today's world allows us to be so much more.

This segued into the importance of your environment. You have to combat the epigenetic effects of the harsh slave environments of years ago, as well as the negative poverty mindset you were raised in if you came from nothing. You do this by changing your environment. That includes changing your friends and your way of speaking. Speak your destiny into existence; your words influence your environment. Inventory your time, your friends, and the rest of your environment and see what needs to be cleansed and what needs to be added. Ride through million-dollar neighborhoods. Read publications like *Worth*, *Bloomberg*, or *Robb Report*. Learn how to talk the talk so you won't lose a step as you begin to walk the walk. Part of walking the walk is expanding your means. You can't become wealthy off your current level of income. You have to expand your means, and you can't do that by budgeting. That's why I made my case as to why budgets absolutely, positively suck.

In the last third of the book, I wanted to get into the nitty-gritty after we tilled the land in the first two thirds. But I couldn't start without helping you discover your bankable purpose. We took a moment to look within, question what we liked and why, and hopefully, I put you on the track to understanding exactly what it is that you were put here to do. I hope you've thought of something that will be in line not only with what you love but also what you're good at. I hope this because it is that thing which will allow you to bring the greatest utility to the greatest number of people without burning yourself out along the way.

We moved from an introspective discussion to a lesson on some of the rules of the money game. Finances have their own language and their own set of rules. It is your responsibility to participate in your own rescue by not only learning the rules of the financial game but also by mastering them.

After that, we went into recognizing opportunity. It is so important that you educate yourself and adjust your vision to be able to see opportunity in all things. Being able to see these opportunities is the difference between the wealthy market drivers and the sheep who follow along at the mercy of whatever the current trend is.

I also talked about the necessity of being able to pivot. You have to be ready and willing to deviate from a plan and to roll with the punches. If you are serious about your dream, you have to be serious about what you are willing to do to make it happen. Keep the end in mind always, but don't let that make you too proud to adjust your plans. The world is constantly changing; therefore, we must also constantly change.

I wanted to end by talking about some things that can help us recognize opportunity. Cycles and bubbles are moving and taking shape around us, and around the world, every day. Educate yourself on these phenomena so that you can position yourself to profit from them. I want to be on the right side of history, the winning side of history, and this book was one of the many steps I try to take every day to bring as many people along with me as I can.

There is a lot of value in this book. I know that because I am a living example of it. But it takes one key ingredient that I can't give you, and that is YOU. You need to give your commitment, your focus, and your participation. The wealthy are willing to do what others won't. If you are content with where you are in life, that is fine; I'm happy for you. But for those of you who feel destined for more, reading this book was an important first step. You were created to bring value to the world. That may be within the confines of an established company, or it may be in the form of your own company or brand. Neither one is better than the other, and not everyone was created to be a business owner. However, even if you are simply looking to be the best employee you can be at a company you love, you need to apply these rules and exercises so that you can make yourself invaluable to that company. You have to create your own opportunities at that company and show them why you are a resource that simply isn't expendable, even in the face of globally shifting tides and artificial intelligence.

To all of my entrepreneurs, those who are ready to create their own opportunity in the market, your mindset and your versatility are your most powerful weapons. Do not be afraid to fail because that means you are afraid to learn. Learning is a process that should never end. Even Tony Robbins and Oprah still go to mastermind groups. Everyone takes their privates jet to them. It doesn't matter how far you ascend; the wealthy realize that there is always more they could be doing because as long as there is still someone out there who you can touch or help with your product or service, your job isn't done. I want everyone like me—anyone who was told that "people like them" don't go to college, anyone who hasn't yet succeed in life, or anyone who has been put down for simply wanting more—to see what is possible, and then to take action to seize it.

You have a purpose that you can leverage to reach financial freedom. Do not bury your talents and waste what you were given. You can establish wealth systems. You can learn the secrets of the wealthy and pass them on to the next generation. You are smart enough to invest, to own land, and to own companies. You were born to be successful. You were born to multiply.

WEALTH COACH | SPEAKER | WEALTHPRENEUR® | ACCOUNTANT

As one of the nation's leading experts on the art of activating wealth potential, *Financial Architect*, entrepreneur, and chief financial officer **LASHAWNE HOLLAND** is Founder of **The Wealthy Leaders Institute** and Chairman of **LaShawne Holland International® (a dba of Holland & Holland Enterprises, LLC)**, a financial development and wealth activation education company focusing on financial literacy education, money mindset mastery, economic elevation, wealth empowerment, innovative business systems education, and peak investment cycle performance strategies.

She is the author of *Wealth Covenant for Couples and founder of The Wealthy Revolution Live Event™ and The Money Made Easy Masterclass Network™*.

Some of her most popular presentation topics include:

- Money Made Easy: Igniting Your Own Economy
- Women of Worth & Wealth in the Marketplace
- Gender Differences in Wealth Accumulation
- Collegepreneur: Creating Your Cash Flow Patterns for Prosperity
- Teenpreneur Titans: Raising Young Business Moguls

- The Treasurer's Masterclass: Training Next Generation Non-Profit CFOs
- The Voice of Money

As a revolutionary and inventive woman in the world of personal finance, she is also **President** of **Finergy, Inc., a financial services company, and the owner of Holland & Holland Enterprises, LLC** – a full-service wealth activation company responsible for educating, empowering, and elevating the personal currency mapping of women of means in the marketplace (www.lashawneholland.com). She is Founder of the Wealthy Revolution Live Event, an annual women's wealth development summit.

Her successes in the real estate market and the business marketplace took her from financial turmoil to financial freedom. She has worked with some of the nation's largest mega-churches, establishing herself as an expert and go-to person for non-profit profitability strategies, ministry corporate infrastructure, and executive compensation best practices. Ministries from all across the nation attend her Treasurer's Masterclass®, an intensive training program for non-profit directors of finance.

The 2015 Godfidence Institute Speakerpreneur of the Year Award recipient and having been named on the Trademark Who's Who list of accomplished women in business, she was also presented with the distinguished ME University 2012 Brand of the Year Award. She is a graduate of the **Morgan State University School of Business and Management** and has worked with the United States Department of Treasury and other government agencies to assist them in planning, implementing, managing, and controlling all financial activities of the company.

As a rising financial columnist and commentator, LaShawne has been featured in over 350 media outlets, including Fox 5 News, BET, Black Enterprise Magazine, BRAVO, CBS News, ABC, NBC, The CW, Yahoo Finance, MarketWatch, The Money Show, Bloomberg Businessweek, Beyond the Dow, Atlanta Business Chronicle, Reuters, Dealbreaker, WORTH, Boston's Business Journal, EMoney Daily, and the Chicago Business Journal, to name a few. She also regularly provides commentary for *Gospel Today Magazine*. Subscribe to her e-zine at www. LASHAWNEHOLLAND.com.

CPSIA information can be obtained
at www.ICGtesting.com
Printed in the USA
BVHW030042200819
556260BV00001B/1/P

9 781728 309385